# SOPHIE AND ME

# Sophie and Me:

▼

## Some of These Days

*Lois Young-Tulin*

iUniverse.com, Inc.
San Jose  New York  Lincoln  Shanghai

Sophie and Me:
Some of These Days

Published by iUniverse.com, Inc.

For information address:
iUniverse.com, Inc.
5220 S 16th, Ste. 200
Lincoln, NE 68512
www.iuniverse.com

ISBN: 0-595-17037-4

Printed in the United States of America

In Memory of Sophie Tucker  1884-1966

# ACKNOWLEDGEMENTS

For my mother, Marion Young, 1910-2001

I am infinitely grateful to my agent, James Schiavone, who, with supreme competence and confidence, did for me what I never could have done for myself. Leslie Friedman-Rifkin helped me to begin and saw me through. Ruth Tulin Cion early on believed in this book and researched relevant Hartford newsclips. Stephen Bressler, whose talent at hairdressing is only surpassed by his love of Broadway musicals. Peter Rothenberg, Peter Lesnik, and Barry Weitz, always available with good advice and professional acumen. My sister, Judith Young-Mallin, whose enthusiasm and love cheered me on. My colleague Gloria Simmons-Bush for her enthusiastic response to early drafts. My three children, Karen Erlichman, Daniel East, and Billy Mann, and my step-son Barak Tulin, all of whom vouched for my sanity and saw me through. My guru, Richard Longchamps, a faithful pen pal and teacher. And last but never least, my husband, David Tulin, who is, among other fine things, the best reader I know.

# CONTENTS

# PART ONE

# CHAPTER I

▼

# SETTING THE STAGE

From the 1950s until her death in 1966, Sophie Tucker played an important role in my life. I was part of her *mishpucha*, and Cuz Sophie, as she signed most of her letters to me, took me under her wing as I journeyed from home...from childhood to adolescence and from adolescence to adulthood.

The fabulous Sophie Tucker received rave notices for her work in television, motion pictures, and night clubs. I put on a record of her night club songs, a choice selection of the spicy sophisticated numbers she sang. The songs capture the zing and excitement of her provocative in-person delivery. Sophie sings with her bouncy exuberance and unerring good taste, poking good natured fun at her own advancing years and king-size proportions with such stimulating ditties as *I'm Having More Fun Since I'm Sixty, How Am I Ever Going To Grow Old,* and *You Can't Deep Freeze a Red Hot Mama.*

As the music plays, I sort through Sophie's letters and cards, as well as some old family photographs. I regret the many photographs and letters lost over the passing years. The memories, however, are stored in my head. It is the time to rake up the coals of the past and share them with others. Scenes and remembered conversations come back to me. I see before me the warm, soft, outspoken matriarch of my father's family, smiling knowingly as she flicks an ash from her cigarette.

"Stop beating around the bush, Lois. Tell your story already. Trust your memory. Take a chance, and stop procrastinating. When you finish the first chapter, you and I are going to play a serious game of gin before Brother gets here. By the way, your hair looks a hundred times better, dear, since I made you cut it."

I dip into my memory bank; yet, my memories are only part of the story of this journey back in time to my relationship to Sophie…it is also a journey forward as I watch some of today's female entertainers who model their image after Sophie Tucker, and who, in fact, benefited from her trailblazing in the entertainment industry. Women who combine multimedia performances acting, singing and telling jokes on stage, in the movies, on television and in night clubs and who are not reticent about using the double entendre.

Sophie was bold and brazen, outspoken and independent. She was a big, brash pioneer whose belting voice and bawdy humor blazed a trail…breaking taboos and traditions that opened doors for all women entertainers and comics who followed. In her own time…which spanned decades…Sophie Tucker violated all the commandments for good Jewish girls. She talked dirty in public. She was a maverick, a feminist ahead of her time who extended the boundaries of comedy and entertainment by women.

Without Sophie Tucker, there could not have been a Carol Channing, a Joan Rivers, a Bette Midler, or perhaps Roseanne. Without Sophie Tucker, opportunities for women would have been far fewer. And far more limited.  And if there had never been a Sophie, America would have had to create her.

Like many career women today, Sophie, when it was not acceptable, was faced with choosing between motherhood and her career. She had given birth to a son before leaving home to make her way in show business and traveling from her Hartford, Connecticut home to New York City. Child care or day care centers were unheard of at the time. Sophie left her infant son in the care of her family...her parents and her sister Annie, a decision that would haunt her throughout her lifetime. At the time, her early marriage to Louis Tuck was on the rocks, and Sophie had to choose between her life's calling as an entertainer and traditional motherhood.

Throughout her years of success, her son Bert was always on her mind, and she saw him as often as possible, given her busy travel schedule. Each week part of her paycheck, even during those lean early years, was sent to Hartford to care for him and to help her aging, hard working parents. Today, show business mothers have more child care options, and resources to keep their children at home with them under the care of paid help. Sophie's family was her childcare agency, but her absence in her son's day-to-day life cost her an emotional price, one from which neither Sophie nor Bert truly recovered.

Sophie was wise about giving advice to the lovelorn; however, as a woman of many contradictions, she herself endured three divorces, and said about her love life, "It is one area in which I have not been able to claim success." Yet her songs are filled with advice to lovers, and she turned her own heartaches into lyrics that made fun of her own personal life and boasted of her success with men.

Like her songs, her voice, her personality, her gowns, Sophie Tucker's life was unique. Hers is the story of a woman with an indomitable will to succeed, whom no obstacle could halt, no handicap could discourage, and no failure could defeat.

With access to never-before-revealed facts, personal letters, family photographs, and personal experience, I will paint a detailed, personal portrait of Sophie Tucker that few rarely, if ever, knew or saw.

As I explore Sophie Tucker's influence on the women entertainers of yesterday and today, I hope to celebrate the women of tomorrow. With

Sophie no longer here to tell her tale, and with the members of her generation disappearing, I am compelled to write this book.

Historically, her past is interwoven with my past. Sophie, herself, revealed her past in her 1945 autobiography *Some of These Days*. Throughout this book, biographical quotes appear, paraphrased from her autobiography, and introduce each chapter. In this way, I attempt to juxtapose Sophie's roots with the more contemporary story being told about Sophie and me.

If we do not use our past, learn from it, take from it all we can, it will have been wasted. Sophie Tucker was a survivor. A funny, strong, independent woman at a time when women weren't supposed to be any of those things; she took great risks, endured great pain and loss, and made a lasting contribution to American culture. The women of today, and especially all those yet to come, owe her a great debt, and stand to gain a great deal from her story. If she could do it, why can't they.

# CHAPTER 2

▼

# GUESS WHO'S COMING FOR DINNER

*January 13, 1884: In a somewhere house on a nowhere road weaving out of Russia toward Poland, the Baltic Sea and America, Mama Kalish unburdened herself of a burbling babe with a belligerent bawl that might have been heard 'round the world...and later was. Papa, forsaking military service to reach out for a better life for himself and family in the new Promised Land, had seized the passport and identity of an Italian AWOL buddy who died en route to America. Reunited, the Kalish family managed to pass muster with United States Immigration officials who stamped them all, forevermore, the Abuzas.*

I grew up in the New York City suburb of Mount Vernon. My childhood was relatively commonplace, with one exception. There was a celebrity in my family. My father had a passion for show business, and his claim to fame in my eyes was that Sophie Tucker was his relative.

I never met my paternal grandmother, although early on family members looked at me and said, "She's the image of Yetta!" Most of my cousins, and even my older sister, were named after Yetta. There was Cousin Janet, and Cousin Joyce, and my sister Judith…all named with a "J" in honor of Yetta. Yet I was the one, they said, who reminded them of her.

There was no question that my father was enamored of show business. He had worked his way through law school in the 1930s by ushering at the Strand Theater in New York and selling candy at the concession stand. Judith and I loved hearing him tell his Strand Theater stories.

"Peanuts, popcorn, chocolate covered almonds!" he'd hawk for us when we begged him to and tell us the story of how he got fired when he climbed to the theater balcony and dripped a glass of water on a patron in the orchestra section who had been rude to him.

A large Hardman piano dominated the living room of our second floor apartment. I liked nothing better than to sit on the wooden piano bench and pretend to be singing to a cabaret audience while I banged the keys. My father knew the words to many show tunes. After dinner, he would turn the pages while I read from sheet music, and played songs from shows like "Guys and Dolls," "Annie Get Your Gun," "Gypsy," "My Fair Lady," and earlier ones like "The Girlfriend." One bonus of his job at the Strand had been that he got to see all the shows free, albeit repeatedly.

It didn't matter that we both sang slightly off key; we had passion and pizzazz and sang and shmaltzed our way through a dozen songs a night while my mother and older sister were in the kitchen doing the dishes.

My dream was to become a big star one day…singing, acting, doing anything that would get me on that big stage at Radio City Music Hall; however, I knew my talent was limited, and was satisfied fantasizing that our living room was the stage and the sound of running water coming from the kitchen the thunderous applause of an adoring audience.

We were still living in that second floor apartment on Beekman Avenue in Mount Vernon the evening my father came home and broke the news.

"Well, it finally happened," he said, winking at me.

I sat on my parents' bed while he emptied the loose change from his trouser pockets and removed his tie. "Guess who came into my office today?"

"Eddie Fisher," I ventured.

"Right field, wrong voice," he said.

"A singer?"

"Not exactly. Let's say the brother of a singer."

"Male or female?" I asked.

"Did you ever see a female brother?"

"I mean the singer," I said.

"Female," he said, changing into a flannel shirt. He buttoned the last button and closed his eyes, threw back his head and belted out, "Some of these days, you're gonna miss…"

"Gawd, really? Sophie Tucker? Did you tell her you're related to her? What happened?" I said.

"Hold on, hold on. Her brother, Moe Abuza, came to see me. The name had been in my appointment book for a month when it rang a bell. Abuza…that was the name of some of my mother's people. Then, Moe came in, and it turned out he had a tax question about Sophie's finances. Moe is Sophie's business manager," my father explained.

"Did he know who you were?" I asked.

"When I told him he did. He was very excited. Most of their people have died, and the family is small. He was very emotional and immediately picked up the telephone and called Sophie. Sophie, Moe and I are having lunch next week."

"What did she sound like on the phone? Was her voice husky and dramatic?" I asked.

"She sounded *hamisha*, like family. No airs. She said she remembered my mother and that my mother had helped her run away from Hartford. You should have seen Moe, puffing a fat cigar. He had tears in his eyes. He was thrilled, he said, to learn that his new lawyer was *mishpucha*."

Later, at the dinner table, I asked my sister, "Guess who Daddy spoke to?"

My sister threw out some wild guesses ranging from the school princi-
pal to our latest teenage idols, Debbie Reynolds and Eddie Fisher. None
was correct.

"Moe Abuza!" my father finally said, unable to contain his secret any
longer.

"Moe who?" Judith asked, giggling. "Who the hell is that?"

"Sophie Tucker's brother and business manager," he said, and then he
told us how since he had begun acquiring clients from the entertainment
field...names like Victor Borga and Helen Hayes...his name had been
given to Moe by Sophie's lawyer and close friend, a guy named Halpern.
"Halpern told them that I was the tax attorney they should consult. So..."
my father concluded, "before I reviewed the papers he had brought me, I
said, 'Moe, I have to tell you something...we're related!'" Daddy paused
for effect.

My sister was hanging on his every word now. "What did he say. Tell us!"

"Well, I explained that our mothers were first cousins, and Moe said he
remembered my mother, Yetta. Then he asked to use my telephone. He
called Sophie. She and I talked. She cried and laughed. It was amazing."

About two weeks later my father made an announcement. "Moe Abuza
is coming for dinner this Sunday!"

"With Sophie?" I asked.

"Not this time. He's coming alone. There'll be plenty of time in the
future for Sophie and the rest of Moe's family to visit with us."

I suspected that my parents were up to having Moe come, but were
embarrassed by our working class neighborhood if Sophie herself were
to visit.

I remember that first dinner with Moe. I was at my chubby, adolescent
stage. When Moe saw me, he squeezed my cheek and said, "Oh, she looks
like her Cuz Sophie...*zaftig* and pretty."

I blushed and wanted to hide under my chair.

Moe was a wonderful dinner guest. He told divine Sophie stories and
stories about the Yanowich and Abuza families in Hartford, where he and

Sophie had spent most of their childhood. Yanowich was my father's family name and ours before he legally changed it to Young when I was in kindergarten.

When Moe left that night he took a long look at me, a chubby little over-emotional eight year old and said again, "This one is like her Cousin Sophie!"

My father's first meeting with Sophie occurred one week later, when he went to her Park Avenue apartment to save her a trip to his office, and to have some time alone with her. Sophie served him hot tea and cookies. Before they got down to looking at the legal papers, he asked Sophie how well she remembered his mother.

Sophie's eyes got teary. "She was my Mama's favorite and one of mine, too. She was my confidante when I plotted to elope with my first husband, Louis Tuck."

My father sat forward in his chair. "She was a special lady, wasn't she?" he said.

"And I believe that she sent you to me," Sophie said. "We're *mishpucha*; I know you'll take good care of me."

"You bet I will," my father said.

Sophie invited my parents to come see her perform at a New York nightclub. After the show, Sophie sat at a card table with a stack of her books, *Some of These Days*, her autobiography. She signed book copies as they were sold. Next to her was one of Moe's old cigar boxes. As people gave her money and checks, she put them into the box.

My parents waited at a table near the exit until the crowd left. Sophie packed up her belongings and pulled up a chair and sat between them.

"Well, guys, how did you like my show?" she asked.

"Wonderful, wonderful, Sophie, but tell me something," my father said, "what were you doing with that cigar box?"

"That's where I put the money I get for my books," Sophie said.

"Then what?" he asked.

"I take it home. What, Milt? What do you want to know, for God's sake?" she said.

"What you're doing is illegal, Sophie. Tomorrow I'll come over and set up an accounting ledger for you. The IRS will need an accounting of your sales receipts. You must keep a record of your sales," he explained.

"Oy vay," Sophie said. Then she grinned. "It's a good thing you came into my life or I'd end up in jail. I had no idea!"

# CHAPTER 3

▼

# MOVIN' ON UP

*Sophie Tucker began life as Sonya Abuza, one of four children born to Jewish emigrants from Europe, who landed in Boston, shortly before the advent of the Gay Nineties. Then Papa bought an unassuming eatery in Hartford, Connecticut, facing the Connecticut River, and the Abuzas moved to Hartford. Sophie's father turned the eatery into a small kosher restaurant, which was patronized by show folks. As a child, Sophie bore her share of the family burden by serving the meals, which her mother cooked.*

*Sophie found she could earn a chubby fistful of change in the crowded hours by booming a clutch of heart-rending ballads, including "Just Break the News to Mother." Sometimes a customer from the nearby Poli's Theater would note the budding singer's powerful projection and potential. The famous vaudeville entertainer Willie Howard, in particular, urged Sophie to contemplate a singing career.*

*Encouraged, Sophie attended Saturday matinees where she looked, listened and began to learn. Contact with the elegant personages from the theatrical world sowed the seeds of discontent with her own drab existence and sent her to bed with haunting dreams of becoming a stage star.*

*One day, while waiting on a group of actors, she impulsively broke into song. The amused stage folk dropped their knives and forks to applaud. Thereafter, patrons at Abuza's Home Restaurant got a one-girl floorshow with their meals.*

Thoughts of my meeting Sophie were tabled until 1953 when my parents invited Sophie, Moe and his wife Blanche and their son Charles for dinner at our new, one-family house on the north side of Mount Vernon. I was afraid that Sophie's arrival would make me the laughing stock of our new neighborhood. I pictured her appearing at our house in one of her long glitzy silver gowns, long silk handkerchief and gaudy headdresses and embarrassing me in front of the neighbors. How well I could picture it, hadn't I, after all, done a Sophie imitation for the camp talent show over the summer, and won second prize for my impersonation of the "Last of the Red Hot Mammas?"

The evening of the "Big Dinner" Judith and I helped my mother set the dining room table with our best china and silverware. My mother cooked our typical Friday night meal of chicken soup, roast chicken with her fabulous stuffing, salad, green beans, baked potatoes and my maternal grandmother's best home-made desserts…apple pie and lemon meringue pie.

The telephone was ringing off the hook once word spread through my new gang of friends that a celebrity was coming to my house for dinner. My best friend Janice and I planned it so that she would call after Sophie arrived, anticipating that she would be able to hear Sophie's famous deep voice in the background when we talked. My friends' image of Sophie came from photographs they had seen of her in entertainment magazines…photographs of Sophie in long, seductive tinsel laden dresses. In her last appearance on the Ed Sullivan Show, Sophie had sported a long handkerchief, which she bandied about with dramatic flair.

The car pulled up in front of our house. My father opened the door for Sophie and escorted her up the front path to the door where my mother waited to be introduced. After Sophie and my mother exchanged hugs my father turned to me.

"This is my daughter, Lois," my father said.

"Hi," I said, offering my hand. Sophie took it.

"Hello, Lois," she said.

I can clearly recall how she looked at that first meeting, her skin, her features. But more than anything, I remember her eyes, clear and piercing, with a striking sense of alertness. Sophie's eyes lingered on me a moment, a quiet smile offered silently before she turned away. Sophie arrived wearing a light blue cotton shirtwaist dress, low heeled shoes and no jewelry to speak of save for a sporty looking wristwatch.

She and Moe had booming voices that monopolized most of the conversation that evening. Moe kidded me about my now slim, developing figure. "This one's just like you, Sis," he said to Sophie, pointing to me. "She'll knock over the guys...full of energy and that strong family will."

I felt myself blush.

I tried not to stare at Sophie and focused on Blanche as we sat down for dinner. Blanche was the oddest of the lot, rumored to be a semi-invalid with a heart condition, and very quiet. It was immediately apparent that Sophie had taken on the job of guiding Charles's life. It almost appeared as if Sophie and Moe were raising Charles, as if they were the parents. Blanche was a full, dark woman with tons of red, red rouge on her cheeks, a dyed black wig, a black silk dress and lots of heavy gold jewelry. She kept mopping at her face with a white handkerchief that she kept stuffed in her cleavage.

Charles was about four years my senior, tall, heavy set, with a blond crew cut and a beefy, pimply face. He carried himself like a soldier, in a military stance, and seemed ill at ease. Sophie made it clear from the beginning that it was my job to show Charles a good time. Janice, as promised, called while we were eating dinner, and I spoke to her just long enough for her to detect Sophie's low guttural voice in the background.

My memory of that dinner is very clear, although the actual dinner conversation is a fuzzy distant memory in the dark recesses of my brain. I vaguely remember my father and Sophie reminiscing about the family. Sophie insisted that it had been grandmother Yetta who had helped her elope with Louis Tuck, the gas station attendant from West Hartford, when she was in her late teens, an escapade that had taken her forever from her home, given her a son, and pushed her into a career in New York City that went from the bottom straight up to major stardom.

Sophie asked my sister about her plans when she finished high school.

"I want to go to college," Judith said.

"Good, good," Sophie said. "It's important to get an education."

Judith smiled, glad to have pleased Sophie. "I'm thinking about applying to schools outside of this area. I want to live in a dormitory."

Sophie nodded. "I approve of that. Moe and I are sending Charles to a boarding school, right Charles?"

Charles nodded and said, "Yes, Auntie."

"I'm thinking about applying to Syracuse or some college in upstate New York," Judith continued.

"That's fine. Not too far away, but far enough so that you have a chance to experience life out on your own," Sophie said.

"Me, too," I said, feeling left out.

Sophie gave me one of her broad grins. "Really? And where will you go?"

"Maybe California," I said, not knowing why I picked California, but glad to be part of the conversation.

"I don't think so, young lady," Sophie said. "It's too far from your family. Family is very important, remember that. You have some time, yet. Think more about staying on the East Coast. I regret that I never went to college, but I got an education from the school of hard knocks…that's for sure."

At the end of the meal, my father led Sophie and my mother into the living room for a cup of coffee. Sophie's sparkling eyes, quick wit and tongue, and definite star quality presence won me over. I thought that Sophie and I hit it off major time. I suspect that my youth and my obvious interest in her warmed her feelings toward me. That…and my forced attention to Charles. It was true that he was a major nerd, but I found myself feeling sorry for him. After dinner, at Sophie's urgings, I invited him to escort me outside as I walked the family cocker spaniel.

Charles and I stuttered our way through a conversation as we walked. He was planning to go to law school one day and, therefore, would major in pre-law at college. He was very close to his Aunt Sophie, I quickly learned, and he talked about her most of the time. "Sophie this and Auntie that…" I asked him if he was close to his mother and father.

"My mother's okay, but she's usually not feeling well and defers to Sophie and Dad on any major decisions that affect my life. Sophie's like a mother to me," he said with obvious emotion.

When we returned from our walk, everyone was sitting in the living room eating pie and drinking coffee. There was a pair of winged armchairs on either side of the wood paneled fireplace. Sophie sat in one chair, and my father sat in the other. Sophie's very presence did that, I was to learn, unseated the usual female head of the household and replaced her. It was something Sophie was not aware of doing; it just seemed to happen naturally. My mother sat on the end of a matching love seat, facing them. Blanche was next to her, facing no one in particular, concentrating, it seemed, on balancing her coffee cup on her lap. The only emotion I caught on Blanche's face was her delight at seeing her son when we returned.

Sophie put out her hand and drew Charles to one side of her and me to her other side. My sister, eminently more sophisticated than I, had disappeared into her room to talk on the telephone. Sophie turned her attention to me and her pride and joy, Charles. "Did you two have a good walk?" she boomed, her smile warm and oh so beautiful.

"We did, Auntie," Charles said.

"Well, Sis, I knew these two would have lots to talk about," Moe boomed.

The members of Sophie's immediate family called each other by their relational names. Moe called Sophie Sis or Sister; Sophie called Moe Brother; Charles called Sophie Auntie; they called Bert, son. However, Sophie called her nephew Charles…not Chuck or Charlie, but the formal Charles, as did his parents.

Moe and my father were puffing on their cigars and beaming as Charles and I found seats and took our places among the elders gathered in the living room. The conversation got around to the Abuza, Yanowich family members who weren't present. My father's two sisters, Rose and Charlotte, were due to arrive at our house soon.

I tuned out the sound of my father's voice. Sophie was focused on the conversation, and I took the opportunity to take a long look at her. She was handsome, I concluded, and had presence. Her make-up was so subtle that her peaches and cream complexion and rosy cheeks seemed natural. Her hair was softly waved, blond and healthy looking.

"I think about little Aunt Sophie sometimes," Sophie said.

"And little Uncle Charlie," Moe added.

"Ah, yes," my father said. By way of explanation he said to my mother, "Little Aunt Sophie and little Uncle Charlie were my mother's baby sister and brother. They must be up in their late eighties now. I can find out. Little Aunt Sophie's son Irving and I have stayed in touch. I know little Aunt Sophie is still alive, but I don't know about little Uncle Charlie. You know, Soph, they haven't spoken to each other in over fifty years. They had some type of falling out years ago and haven't spoken to each other since."

"Unheard of," Sophie said, clearly upset. She took a sip from her cup, her eyes peering just over the rim, sharp and evaluating, as if her mind ceaselessly sifted the material that passed through it, allowing this, dismissing that, her sense of judgment oddly final from which there could be no appeal. "Milton," she said to my father, "It's up to us, you and me, to do something about this! The *mishpocha* need to meet. It's time for a family reunion."

The remainder of the evening Sophie and my father planned and plotted. Sophie was adamant in her desire to hold a family party. She was like that; once her mind was made up there was no stopping her.

When Rose and Charlotte arrived my father introduced them to Sophie and Moe and Blanche and Charles. My aunts suddenly got shy and looked a bit star struck. But after a short time they too were drawn into the plot. By the end of the evening, Moe, Sophie, my father, Rose and Charlotte were throwing out ideas, names and rumors about their long lost relatives...soon, it seemed, to be reunited in this very same room... our living room.

What stuck with me about the discussion was the fact that bitter things happened in families. So many years ago little Uncle Charlie and little Aunt Sophie spoke angry words. Hurt was inflicted. Those things happened among friends, too, but that was different. People were more vulnerable where family was concerned. The angry words were hotter; the hurt was more painful. Silences grew to become as obtrusive as the most bothersome of family members. Breaking the silence was the challenge. It would take strength, and in this instance, it would mean dealing with pride and with fear.

# CHAPTER 4

▼

# PREPARATIONS

*Sophie was a big, buxom child, physically and emotionally matured beyond her years. While still in her early teens she succumbed to the wooing of the neighborhood "dream-boat" and in 1900 she fell hard for Louis Tuck, a handsome young catch across the way. One day, they sneaked off and were married.*

*She returned from her elopement to announce, to her family's consternation, that she had become Mrs. Louis Tuck. Before the almost child bride's own child came, they had moved in with her folks, where she was always needed.*

*Determined to escape the drudgery that was aging her parents, Sophie gave Louis a choice: an independent life with a home of their own, or else. The gap widened. Her marriage and early motherhood, to any ordinary girl, would have meant the end of dreams and aspirations to a stage career. But Sophie was no ordinary girl. When the honeymoon waned, and it became evident that her hasty marriage held little more than a continuation of the drudgery in the restaurant, she took tearful leave of her baby son, packed her meager belongings and boarded a train for New York.*

*Making it in New York was her goal. She haunted songwriters in Tin Pan Alley. Hope faded, and with funds shrinking she asked the proprietor of Café' Monopol to let her literally sing for her supper. He asked her name.*
*"Sophie Tucker," she improvised.*

When I entered highschool, my friends enjoyed nothing better than to watch my imitation of Sophie Tucker singing *Some of These Days*. During the summer of 1956, at summer camp in the Berkshires, one of my claims to fame was the imitation I did of Sophie. Standing on my cot, I entertained my bunkmates by belting out a throaty version of her songs. On the first talent show night, I won first place for my rendition of *My Yiddishe Mamme*.

That same summer, my parents accompanied Sophie and Moe on her European tour. Sophie was playing in Paris, London and Rome. I received postal cards from all three cities signed "Cuz Sophie." Thus began a correspondence and friendship that would span the years of my teens through to my years as a young mother.

At the end of that summer, with camp over, I returned home to the news that Sophie alone was coming to spend a whole weekend at our house. They were still planning on a family reunion, but, according to my father, it would take some research so that they could include as many family members as they could locate. That reunion probably wouldn't take place for a year or two the way things were going.

My sister was accepted at Syracuse University, and in September I was the only kid at home, the telephone all to myself. And now, Sophie was coming for a long weekend, and would sleep across the hall from my bedroom in my sister's room.

What excitement in our house. My mother redecorated my sister's room, buying a pink bedspread and new throw pillows. The bathroom that Judith and I had shared was transformed in appearance with fluffy guest towels trimmed with pink poodles and a coordinated set of tissue box holder, waste paper basket and drinking cup. Mom selected a design that she thought Sophie would like…a glitzy imitation of her bejeweled, bedecked stage persona. The three piece ensemble was painted gold with a scene hand-painted on each item that depicted the Eiffel Tower, a long rhinestone dog's leash that ended with a pink poodle wearing a rhinestone collar. Tacky, I thought, but it did dress up the bathroom that Sophie and I would share.

Moe came to the house for dinner the night before, on a Thursday, to look over Sophie's accommodations. He pinched my cheek, turned me around by the waist and said, "She sure takes after her Cuz Sophie."

That night Moe ate as if he hadn't eaten in days, stopping only to compliment my mother on her cooking. Moe was no taller than my father but a decade older with that gravelly voice and a full red nose. Each time he referred to Sophie as Sis, I thought of how Judith and I had begun to correspond while she was at college, addressing each other as "Sis" as a way to make fun of Sophie and Moe.

When I got home from school on Friday, the caterers were carrying into the house trays of Jewish delicatessen treats while my mother and grandmother were in the kitchen making matzah ball soup, kreplach, potato latkes, all the traditional foods that my father loved and that they assumed Sophie would love, too. They were offering her home cooking, food like her Yiddishe Mama used to make.

The slip covers on our living room furniture were sent out for a cleaning; a rug cleaning service came in and brought new life into our drab green carpet, and the crystal and silver were polished to a glitter. My mother supervised the renovations with my father walking behind her, voicing his preferences and urging her to spare no expense for this momentous celebrity weekend visit.

I told my friends about Sophie's expected visit, but my parents forewarned me not to invite a bunch of my friends over since Sophie needed a restful weekend in the country, not a fan club invasion.

My mother made h'or d'oeuvres...pigs in the blanket (the pigs being tiny kosher hot dogs), k'nishes, and chopped liver. I had gobbled up the first batch of pigs in the blanket before Sophie arrived.

"Lois, keep your hands off this next batch," Mom warned. "We'll have nothing left by the time Sophie arrives."

Judith called at that moment, and I croaked "Some of these days..." into the telephone, giving my sister my best Sophie imitation.

"Stop it," Judith whined. "If you make me laugh, I'll wet my pants." She did that when she laughed too hard.

"I wish you were home this weekend," I said, suddenly missing my big sister.

"I do too, Sis," she said. "Give my best to Cuz."

"You should see this place," I said. "Your room is the pink palace, and our bathroom looks like a cat house," I whispered, not wanting to hurt my mother's feelings.

"Well, write me all about it," Judith said. "Let me talk to Mom."

While my mother took the phone, I ran upstairs to get dressed before Sophie arrived.

Around six o'clock a big, black Lincoln pulled up to our house. First Moe got out, beefy faced and red nosed, his booming Abuza voice audible through my closed bedroom window. My father reached in a hand to help Sophie out of the car.

Once again, Sophie appeared, not in a bejeweled evening gown, but wearing low-heeled pumps and a light blue shirtwaist dress. She carried a leather pocket book with her well-manicured pink nails and her hair was neatly coifed, platinum blonde. Sophie stepped onto the curb, holding onto my father's arm.

She looked elegant, sophisticated. In contrast, Moe wore a dark shiny suit, a white on white short sleeve shirt open at the neck and had a curly thick mane of luxurious hair on his head, that looked even lighter next to his ruddy complexion. With his large red nose he seemed almost a male caricature of his sister. Moe's voice was booming again, deep bass, coming from his throat and lungs, a jolly, unpretentious voice and speech pattern.

I ran downstairs and opened the front door to the trio, staring, I'm sure, wide-eyed at Sophie. She was so fleshy and real, and pink and beautiful, and smelled so sweet and clean. All of these thoughts came to me as I grinned up at her smiling face and sparkling eyes. There she was, standing before me, looking even better than I remembered her from her last visit. An energy surrounded Sophie, a vibrancy and engagement that was almost physical.

She stared into my eyes. "She looks like your Mamma," she said to my father. "Yes, she sure does."

Dinner went well. While they ate, the four of them picked up where they had left off and talked about how things were progressing in finding family members for the big reunion. It was then that I learned the exact relationship between Sophie and my father. Daddy's grandmother and Sophie's mother were sisters.

Sophie had two pieces of pie and then volunteered to help with the dishes.

"Don't be silly," my mother said. "Lois will help me."

I stood up and began to clear the table.

I reached for Sophie's plate. She put a well-manicured hand over her dish. "Oh, no you don't. I insist on helping too. It's so nice to be with family. I don't want to be waited on. It reminds me of how sick I am of eating in hotels when I'm on tour."

It was in the kitchen that I got to see another side of Sophie, a more domestic side. My mother washed the dishes; Sophie dried, and I put them away.

"Come on, Milt, you help, too," Sophie called out as my father stuck his head through the kitchen doorway. "I know better than to ask Moe; he's so clumsy in the kitchen," Sophie added. She grabbed my father's arm and threw him a dishtowel. "Come on, now. Marion made that delicious dinner. You help clean up. Go on, Marion, you go inside and keep Moe company while we finish up in here."

I stood with my mouth open watching as Sophie untied my mother's apron strings and led her into the living room where Moe was looking sleepy and nodding off in his chair.

Sophie stormed back into the kitchen. "Milt," she said to my father. "Finish drying these pots. I'll finish drying these dishes, and Lois is putting things away. You know, your own Mama used to get your father to help her in the kitchen," she added, glaring at my father who did not dare protest as Sophie tied the flowered apron around his middle.

"If I had a dollar," Sophie said, "for every greasy dish I have washed in my lifetime, I'd be the richest woman in show business today."

By the time I awakened the following morning, everyone else was up. Still not dressed, I came downstairs and found my parents and Sophie outside on the back patio eating brunch. Moe had gone back home the night before to Blanche and Charles.

Sophie was wearing a flowered bathrobe. Our outdoor wrought iron and glass top table was overflowing with fresh bagels, cream cheese, lox and freshly brewed coffee. I grabbed a bagel and ran upstairs to shower and dress. I was meeting some friends in an hour.

When Janice and Phyllis came by to pick me up, I took them outside to meet Sophie. They were both suddenly shy, and held back at the doorway to the patio.

"Sophie, I want you to meet two of my best friends, Phyllis and Janice, "I said, dragging my two friends towards Sophie.

Sophie immediately tried to put them at ease. "Come on over here so I can meet Lois's friends," she said, "and have a bagel before you go." She motioned them forward. "Come on, come on. I won't bite."

They each grabbed a bagel and lathered it with cream cheese. My father brought out some folding chairs so they could sit down.

I looked at my wristwatch. "We don't have too much time," I said to no one in particular. "We have a party tonight," I said, aiming my explanation at Sophie, "and we're going shopping to find something to wear."

Janice, I noticed, was staring at Sophie, and had absent-mindedly stopped chewing her bagel.

"Come on, Janice," I complained. "Finish up so we can go."

Janice stood and extended a hand to Sophie. "It was a pleasure to meet you. Could I…I mean…would you…"

"Certainly," Sophie said, suspecting that Janice wanted an autograph.

Janice blushed and took out a camera.

"Wait a minute," Sophie said, holding up a hand. "I thought you wanted an autograph. But a photograph so early in the morning. I'm not even dressed. I have no make up on." Meanwhile, Sophie motioned for me to stand beside her. "Aw, go on, uh, Janice, isn't it? Take it fast!" Sophie was laughing now, patient and natural with Janice and her obvious star struck awe of Sophie.

That evening when I went out with my friends, Sophie was in her room napping, so I didn't see her. And later, when I got home from the party, the house was quiet; they were all asleep.

Sunday I caught up with Sophie over another brunch of bagels and lox. It was drizzling outside so this time everyone was in the dining room. I took a seat at the table and greeted everyone.

"So, Lois, how was the party last night?" Sophie asked suddenly.

"It was fun," I said, selecting a sesame seed bagel.

"Were there fellas there?" Sophie asked.

"Yeah," I answered.

"And you? Did you dance a lot?" she persisted.

"I did. I had a great time."

"Do you have a boyfriend?" Sophie asked. I noticed my father frowning.

"Daddy!" I whined. I turned to Sophie. "He doesn't approve of kids my age going steady."

"He's right, you know, but you'll do it anyway. We all did," Sophie said, giving me a tender smile. Then she looked deep in thought for a while. Finally, looking resigned, she said, "I'd like to turn back the clock and redo certain things."

"What things?" I asked. I sensed that if Sophie answered, we would be treading on new ground.

Sophie raised her eyes to mine. "I've always been competitive. I was that way as a teenager. Right from the start, driven to do better and be better. I strode my way to the top, and when I had to climb on other people to get there, I reasoned that that was all that mattered...to establish my name. Success then fueled success. And then there's my family." The eyes that met mine were filled with self-reproach. "My son...my one, single greatest source of shame."

My father patted Sophie's hand and glared at me. "Don't be so hard on yourself," he said.

Sophie might have denied it, might have tried to lighten her shame with empty words, but I had the feeling that she wanted our relationship to be an honest one

After brunch, Sophie and I found ourselves alone in the sun porch. "Let's make a date, you and me, to have you come into the city and go with me to my beauty parlor for a hair cut. What do you say?" Sophie asked.

I ran my fingers through my long dark hair. "You don't like my hair?" I said, suddenly feeling self-conscious.

"It's okay, but in a year or two you'll be off to college. This is the time to experiment with some more sophisticated hairstyles before you decide the look you want at college. You'll want something easy to maintain that looks good on you. You have a lovely face. You don't need all that hair," Sophie said. "Andre is superb! We could make a day of it. You'll come in the night before and sleep over at my place, then we'll go to Andre's the next day. It will be fun."

# CHAPTER 5

▼

# THE HAIRCUT

*A career had begun. Nights of loneliness and heartaches followed days of bitter disappointment in the Big City. But in the small East Side Café Monopol, Sophie got her first job singing for her meals. Friendly song pluggers in Tin Pan Alley had directed her to the German Village, a notorious, all-night hot spot on Fortieth Street near Broadway. Undaunted by repeated rebuffs, she finally persuaded the proprietor to give her a chance. The "big blonde with the big voice"…in reality a girl of sixteen…clicked with the midnight rounders. It proved a lucrative engagement. Back in Hartford the family was amazed at the sums which the prodigal daughter sent home weekly for the care of the baby and to buy gifts for the others.*

Sophie called me on the telephone several days later.

"Now, Lois, you come into the city early. We'll have dinner at my place and you'll stay overnight. Then, the next morning you'll go with me to Andre'. I'm going to supervise your new look," Sophie insisted.

"I don't want my hair cut short," I said.

"Now stop it! You have a beautiful face and too much hair. Trust me. Knowing how to look is my business, right?"

I had to agree.

"Well, enough said. Be at my place at five thirty. Mom or your father will arrange transportation." Sophie usually referred to my parents as Mom or your father; sometimes she'd say your Daddy, which was the way she and Moe talked about their father, followed by *Alav ha'sholem,* which in Yiddish means "peace should be with him." They called their mother Mama, *Alav ha'sholem,* and their father Daddy, *Alav ha'sholem* or Papa, *Alav ha'sholem.* And, of course, they continued to call each other Sis and Brother.

When I hung up the telephone I thought about Sophie and Moe. They laughed a lot together and argued. They were inseparable. Moe began and ended each day with Sophie and filled in the middle hours booking Sophie's acts and managing her affairs. She was his life, and she didn't make a career move without Brother. Charles, it was evident, was the apple of Sophie's eye. At the end of the day, Sophie would say to Moe, "Enough today, Brother. Go home to Blanche, and tell Charles to call me."

I arrived at 737 Park Avenue two days later. The doorman rang upstairs to Sophie's apartment to clear my admittance. I rang the bell to her apartment. A uniformed maid opened the door.

I heard Sophie's deep voice boom out, "In here, Lois."

Sophie was in her private study, a well lit, corner room with double window exposure. A small gold desk with a tiny lamp faced the doorway. Moe was standing in the doorway, puffing a big cigar, talking and gesticulating in his gruff, warm way.

He turned as I entered. "Well, look who's here, Lois, dear." He gave me a big bear hug and planted a wet cigar kiss on my forehead. "So...I hear you and Soph have a big day planned for tomorrow."

"Never mind, don't get her nervous, Brother. Andre and I have big plans for this one. Come here, Loey, and give your Cuz Sophie a proper hello, come on."

She smelled wonderful, of perfumed powder and spices. Sophie's nails were always immaculately groomed and this particular day painted a cherry red. She was wearing a navy skirt and white silk blouse, a string of pearls with matching pearl earrings. She looked like an understated Boston matron. Her ample bosom pressed against me as we embraced. She pushed back my shoulders to get a clearer view of my face. She brushed the hair back from my face with her elegant hands. It gave me an uncomfortable feeling of being exposed, my skin peeled away layer by layer, revealing what lay beneath. I felt my hand toy with the button at my throat. Then Sophie planted a wet kiss on my cheek.

After Moe left, Sophie showed me to a room behind her study, which was to be my room. I sat down on the bed and unpacked the few things I had brought in my overnight case. I could hear Sophie talking on the telephone.

At six-thirty there was a knock at my door. The maid peeked inside. I was lying on the bed reading.

"Dinner is being served. Miss Sophie asked me to come get you."

Sophie and I sat in her dining room at one end of a long formal table. The maid brought us a light supper of sliced white meat chicken, rice, string beans, a salad and some Danish pastry for dessert. As we ate we talked. Sophie seemed pleased that I was there.

"Remember," she said, waving her fork in the air and looking into my eyes. "'Til age eighteen a girl needs good parents...you have them. From eighteen to thirty-five she needs good looks. You have them. From thirty-five to fifty-five a girl needs a good personality. Keep on as you are and you'll fit the bill. From fifty-five on, a girl needs cash. So don't rush into marriage and get all starry eyed about some poor schnook. Okay?"

I smiled. "But my father was poor when my mother married him. I don't think people should marry for money," I said, my head high.

"No...but it helps," she said and laughed.

Then she got serious. "The key is," she added suddenly, "if you are independent and live up to your potential, follow your dreams...it won't matter what your guy is worth. You make it on your own...like I did.

Then you can love anyone you wish. Be independently wealthy or at least comfortable…on your own…and love will not come out of desperation but out of choice. You understand?"

I nodded. I did understand. And her words would stay with me throughout my life. I had never heard anyone say anything quite so odd, and I suppose that it was at that moment I knew that something truly different and wonderful had entered my life.

Sophie's eyes were shining, "Are you up for some gin rummy?"

"Sure," I said.

"I hoped you'd say that. The cards are on the table in the living room."

Sophie shuffled the cards and dealt them. I looked up from my hand. Sophie started organizing her cards. "Have you been dating?" she asked.

I put down the 7 of hearts, and she picked it up before discarding the 2 of clubs. "Yes," I answered. I took the 2 of clubs, and I discarded the 9 of clubs.

Sophie picked from the stack of cards and discarded a 6 of diamonds. "Anyone special?"

I picked a card. "Same guy…Barry," I said.

Sophie discarded. "Keep yourself open to meeting other guys, too," she said.

I didn't reply for a moment. I threw down a 2 of spades. "I know," I said.

Sophie smiled and picked from the stack.

My hand was coming together. Another card and I'd be done.

Sophie threw down the jack of clubs. I paused. I took a deep breath and laid my hand on the table. "Gin!"

After losing, Sophie put away the cards and turned on the television.

We watched television for a half-hour and then went to bed early because Sophie said we had to get up at five o'clock in the morning to get to Andre's before the other customers arrived. Sophie always did it that way. She'd come to Andre's before his salon opened. Sophie's manicurist and hair washer would be there, too, along with Andre himself. They'd give Sophie their full attention, and she didn't have to contend with fans, autographs or the stares of the other customers.

Sophie was already up and dressed when I came out of my room the next morning. I was dressed and ready to go. Sophie was at her desk making out some checks.

"There's some juice and toast for you on the dining room table," she said. "Will that be enough? Would you like an egg, too?"

"No. Toast and juice is fine," I said.

"Are you nervous?" she said, running her gorgeous hands through the ends of my hair.

"Yes! Are you sure—"

She interrupted me. "Loey, you said you'd trust me. Not another word. Some times the most we can give, or get, is trust."

"Okay, truce," I grinned.

A car was waiting downstairs to take us to Andre's on Sixth Avenue near 55th Street. I felt a party to some conspiracy, this early morning voyage, begun before the city was awake, with the streets of New York deserted and the skyline shrouded in mist. We got there by five forty-five. Andre' was already inside, turning on lights, and greeting the manicurist and hair washer who arrived seconds before we did.

Sophie put a smock over her dress and told me to get myself one in the back while she talked privately to Andre. I did just that, and when I came out Sophie was telling Andre the look she wanted for me. If it had been anyone else taking over my appearance like that I would have balked...but I trusted Sophie, and in the car on the way over I had made up my mind to sit back and enjoy it...to give up control and see what happened.

Meanwhile, Sophie was having the works. In a short while she was sitting under the hair dryer, her hair in rollers and clips while the manicurist was doing her nails. I looked at the mirror in front of me while Andre clipped, snipped and combed my hair. I saw through the mirror Sophie winking at me. I grinned to reassure her that I was okay.

My hair was lying on the floor. I looked down when Andre went to get some conditioner, and picked up several locks. I wrapped them in tissue paper from the dispenser on the counter top and slipped the package into my bag. For sentimental reasons, I thought. I could already see that my hair cut was going to work. It was shorter than I was used to, but stylish, curly and layered.

I looked up and in the mirror saw that Sophie was watching. I gave her a thumbs up sign and blew a kiss. She grinned and blinked her pleasure in my satisfaction.

An hour later we stepped outside and into the still waiting car that would take us back to Sophie's apartment.

"I love it," I said, squeezing her hand affectionately.

"It looks marvelous, darling," Sophie said. "Next time you'll not worry and remember that I know what looks best."

When we got back to the apartment, Sophie left me in the living room while she checked her telephone messages.

I admired the large Steinway piano in the far corner of the room. I could hear Sophie busy talking on the telephone in her study when I sat down on the piano bench and opened the mahogany cover, revealing shiny ebony and ivory keys. I hit the middle C. The tone was rich and clear. There was no sheet music around, so I played from memory. I added chords for the left hand and, with my right, playing two octaves at a time, I played the melody to *Someone To Watch Over Me*. I played as I did in the evenings when my father sang along, shmaltzing it up with flourishes and trills. The keys were easy and well tuned. I improvised, losing myself with the old familiar fantasy of playing to a large, admiring audience.

I felt a hand on my shoulder and knew without looking that Sophie had discovered my ridiculous antics. I felt my cheeks grow hot, and stopped playing.

"Don't stop…here," and she put the sheet music to *Some of These Days* on the stand. "Try this."

"Oh…" I stuttered. "I'm not good. I just fool around for fun," I said, feeling as if I had been caught with my hand in the cookie jar.

"No…I like it. Play more," she boomed. It was more an order than a suggestion.

I felt I had no choice. I sight read the melody and improvised with my left-hand chords. "Some of these days," Sophie belted out the words, keeping her hand on my shoulder. "You're going to miss me,"and I accompanied her as she sang her theme song.

I kept up with her pace and the melody with my right hand; however, I faked the left bass notes as I went. When we finished, Sophie threw her arms around my neck and hugged me, then tossed her head back and roared with laughter.

I felt embarrassed, but I found myself laughing with her.

"My mother once bought me a piano, but I refused to practice…my fat fingers couldn't play scales…so Mama sold it. You'll never make it to Carnegie Hall, Lois, unless you learn to read the left hand music, but if Ted Shapiro, my pianist, is ever sick, I'll call on you to fill in," she said, winking playfully.

Her good humor was contagious, and I felt light and joyful. Sophie wiped tears of joy from her eyes. "It's definitely in your blood, though, that old Abuza/Yanowich ham! You have it!"

"So does Daddy," I confided.

"Milton? He doesn't…I mean…"

"I play and he sings along, almost every night after dinner. And we really ham it up…and sing show tunes together. Off tune, of course, but we have a great time," I said.

"I love it! He never said a word," Sophie said.

"He'll probably kill me for telling you," I said. "You know, he's really a frustrated entertainer."

Sophie clasped her hands in front of her with glee. "Well, it will be our secret, Loey. I won't tell him that I know a thing," she said. "Are you hungry? It's lunchtime, and I'm starving. Let's go inside and have a good salad."

I followed her to the dining room where we were served a chef salad, iced tea and rye toast. Dessert was sherbet with fruit salad. As we ate, Sophie spoke to me of what life should be, the heights it should reach, the passions it should embrace, all this said and done, I suspected, in the hope that I might come to live it as a bird on the wing. "For life is best lived," Sophie said, "on the edge of folly."

I wasn't sure what that meant. I had never conceived of my destiny as anything but decided. I would graduate from high school, go to college, have a family. I would do what my mother had done, and her mother before her. I'd find whatever joy or glory there might be in life along the same path they'd trod before me.

The telephone rang as we were finishing our lunch. Sophie excused herself and picked up the telephone in her study. Five minutes later she returned. "It was your father. He's picking you up in fifteen minutes and taking the rest of the day off. Get your things together, although I hate to let you go." She cupped my chin in her hand. "Your hair is divine, honey. You look wonderful. I think I'll wait with you in the lobby so I can see your father's face when he gets a look at the new you."

My father fussed and oohed over my new look and congratulated Sophie on her supervision of my makeover. Sophie and I hugged goodbye, and her clean, sweet smell remained with me as my father and I drove out of the city and north into Westchester County.

# CHAPTER 6

▼

# SISTERS

*Burlesque was then the great school of experience from which many of the biggest stars of our time were graduated into big time vaudeville, musical comedy and the dramatic stage. For Sophie Tucker, too, it was a memorable stepping stone. She toured with a burlesque circuit during which she met a fellow rising star, Fanny Brice, thus beginning a lifelong friendship. Marc Klaw, of the theatrical firm of Klaw and Erlanger, spotted Sophie and talked Ziegfeld into using her in his latest extravaganza. At the Atlantic City try-out, she fractured the seat holders, infuriating star Nora Bayes. Thus, from burlesque Sophie lapsed into Ziegfeld's Follies, only to fall and suffer a broken heart.*

*Yes, on opening night she had stopped the show. Yet when the Ziegfeld Follies of 1909 made the Main Stem, the promising newcomer was ruthlessly pared to one turn. Nora soon left, succeeded by Eva Tanguay, who coveted Sophie's torrid rendition of "Moving Day in Jungle Town." To appease the professional jealousy first of Nora Bayes and then of Eva Tanguay, Ziegfeld fired her. She never appeared in the "Follies" again.*

When Judith was in the middle of her first semester at Syracuse University, she was invited to spend a weekend at Cornell, with a guy who would turn out to be her husband. My parents were against my sister going unchaperoned to visit Joel, but Sophie got wind of it and intervened.

Judith called on a weekend when Sophie was at our house. Judith needed written permission from my parents since it was a trip off-campus.

"Wait a minute…wait a minute!" Sophie boomed, when she heard my father talking on the telephone to Judith. "Let me talk to her."

"Pick up the extension," Daddy told Sophie.

She did. "Judith! Don't worry, darling. Your daddy will let you go if…and only if…you sleep at my sister Annie's house. Annie lives near Cornell, and she'll be the chaperone. That way you can still go off and enjoy your beau and friends at Cornell, but first let me call Annie. We'll call you back."

Annie, it turned out, was the non-show business sibling of the Abuza family. She and her husband lived near Cornell. Annie, it turned out, was a homebody. She baked and cooked and, although she and her husband Jules were childless, was the maternal nurturer of the family.

Annie and her husband had been supported by Sophie financially from the day they were married. Sophie regularly sent the Aronsons money to help them make ends meet. On the one hand, Annie depended on Sophie financially; on the other hand, Sophie depended on Annie emotionally. For Sophie, Annie's home was reminiscent of Jennie Abuza's, their mother, just as Annie's cooking was like their Mama's. Annie had learned to cook in Abuza's Restaurant where Mama had cooked all the meals. It was Annie who had been Bert's surrogate mother after Sophie left home, left Louis Tuck and Son, then just an infant, and gone to New York to make it in show business. Annie and Sophie were very close. In those early years, Annie wrote to Sophie several times a week, wherever Sophie was playing her act there was a letter waiting from Annie. One time when Sophie hadn't heard from Annie for several days, she knew something was wrong. She could feel it.

Sure enough, Sophie received Annie's telegram. "Come home at once," the telegram said. "Pa very low. Love, Annie."

By the time Sophie arrived in Hartford poor Pa was gone. Sophie arrived too late to see Papa alive. If only, Sophie often said, if only she had received Sis's wire a couple of hours earlier, she could have caught the Century and been there in time. After Papa had his fatal stroke and could not move or speak, the family told Papa they had sent for Sophie. Sophie was always Papa's favorite. Pa, Annie later told Sophie, had kept watching the door for Sophie to come until he had finally closed his eyes.

In those early years when Sophie came home to Hartford and Son was a baby, it was clear that Sister Annie was now Son's mama. Sophie felt like a visitor. Son would put his arms around Sophie's neck and hug and kiss her, but then he would squirm to get down and toddle back to Sis.

Several years after Papa died, Sophie made preparations for her first trip to London. Son was away at boarding school that year. Sis was living alone in Hartford where she had a job at the Connecticut Furrier Company. Sophie wrote to Annie and asked if she would like to go with her to London. Back came a letter. Jules Aronson had asked Annie to marry him. Annie wanted to know what Sophie thought she should do.

Sophie thought well of it. She had always liked Jules and remembered him from her teen years in Hartford. She was sure that Jules would be able to give Sis the happiness she needed and deserved. Pa and Ma were both gone. Moe and Phillip were away; Moe lived in Brooklyn, and big brother Phillip was married and starting his own family. That left Annie alone. Sophie had promised Ma before she died and when Annie was raising Son, that she would see that Annie had the grandest wedding any girl ever had. Now Sophie would make good on that promise.

Annie set the date for March 31. As soon as Sophie got back to New York from her London trip, she and Brother Phil started with wedding preparations. Annie came down to shop with Sophie for her trousseau. Day and night the two sisters were on the go. Sophie engaged Chalif's Rooms on West 57$^{th}$ Street for a real kosher wedding and supper. The kind of celebration Mama would have liked. The famous Cantor Jossele Rosenblatt was singing in New York. Sophie rushed over to arrange for him to officiate at the ceremony with Rabbi Aaron.

Two hundred invitations were sent out to all their relatives as far as Boston and Detroit, close family friends, Ma's old friends in Hartford, the mishpocha in Brooklyn and New York, and a large number of Sophie's personal and professional friends. Railroad tickets were sent off to those who couldn't afford to come so far. Hotel quarters were engaged to put up the family, relatives and friends. Nearly every stage dress Sophie owned was sent to those who needed a fine dress for the occasion.

Sophie still could picture Sis in her white lace wedding gown. How beautiful Annie had looked. At the time, Sophie only wished Ma and Pa could have been there to see her. Annie was escorted to Chalif's by Phil and his wife Leah, Moe, and Sophie. Eddie Elkins and his orchestra struck up the Wedding March, and the bridal procession went into the shul for the ceremony. Sophie was the matron of honor. She felt she was taking the place that Ma, if she had been alive, would have had. As Sophie stood under the chuppa (canopy) near Annie, tears blinded her. She sent up a prayer of thanks to God for making that evening possible. Sophie and Annie remained very close after Annie's wedding and her move to Auburn, New York.

So...while my parents and I waited, Sophie went upstairs to call Annie and talk privately. She came downstairs about twenty minutes later, grinning. "Get Judith on the telephone for me," she ordered my father.

Sophie took the phone. "Judith, it's Cousin Sophie. It's all arranged. You'll bring your beau to Annie's house in Auburn," she boomed. And a deal was made.

For the remainder of my sister's stay at Syracuse, my sister raved about Annie. Judith said that Annie was the kitchen queen, that she lived in a simple house in Auburn with a front porch. She said that Annie's husband Jules was quiet and sweet. Annie, she said, loved to be in the kitchen. Judith was learning how to cook all the traditional Jewish dishes like stuffed derma, kasha and bow ties. As Annie cooked she talked with Judith who was falling for Joel.

After that first visit to Annie's, Judith had blanket permission to visit Joel at Cornell via Annie's house. There were about seven such visits. It was a double draw: Judith could see Joel and also could visit with Annie. Judith felt part of the warm family circle, and confided in Annie that she was falling for Joel.

Even though Annie seemed to approve of Joel, Sophie said that she was reserving judgment until she met him in person herself. Sophie fashioned herself the head of the family, now, and considered herself the best judge of someone's character.

# CHAPTER 7

▼

# SUMMER GAMBLIN' GALS

*Sophie retraced her steps to vaudeville to start all over again. Booking agent William Morris planned an American Music Hall circuit for her patterned on the famed English music halls. At a benefit, he gauged the extra magnetism and stage presence that marked Sophie's star quality. He saw a potential head-liner. He booked her into his music hall in Chicago. He added to his roster, and gave this still uncut gem the facets of poise and style. She was comely and warmly appealing, though with an undeniable girth and assertive approach. Still, since most viewers associate the singer with the song, Sophie became iden-tified with the humorous and inoffensive double entendre, with herself as butt of the joke. Her audiences howled and adored her. Sophie didn't sing to shock people; her blues concerned what she called "sex," but not vice.*

*She took the Windy City by storm, and it was there her climb to fame began. The Loop began to buzz with talk about the buxom blonde who rocked the house with her syncopation. Critics lauded her. Jack Lait dubbed her "The Mary Garden of Ragtime." The magic touch of success brought poise and polish and new raiment to enhance Sophie's Junoesque charms; and a black songwriter named Shelton Brooks brought Sophie "Some of These Days."*

*Her success in Chicago, however, was not unmarred by setbacks. Two ventures into musical comedy resulted in no progress, and Sophie went back to vaudeville. Her bookings were on western circuits, far from Broadway, and from one of these trips she returned with a new husband. Louis Tuck had died. Her second husband was a vaudevillian named Frank Westphal. The marriage ended in divorce after the first year.*

*Popular as Sophie Tucker was in Chicago, it was not until the summer of 1914...after playing the Keith Circuit, vaudeville's aristocracy in 1913...five years after her experience in Ziegfeld's Follies that she got her first chance to play the Palace in New York. What she did that week in vaudeville's most famous theater is now stage legend.*

Sophie was an avid gin rummy player. During the summer before my senior year in highschool, I was her favorite gin partner. My job was to make sure, after Moe warned me, that Sophie did not cheat when adding up the scores. I didn't consider it cheating, but preferred to think of it as her ineptitude with numbers.

It was usually during the early days of summer that I saw the most of Sophie. The summer heat got her down, and she preferred to receive guests at her air-conditioned apartment or sit beside the ocean or the swimming pool at Vernon Hills Country Club in Westchester County where my family was a member. That summer, Sophie spent a lot of time at our house to get away from the hot New York City air. We'd play cards at my house or by the pool at the country club.

Sophie insisted that we play for real money, although since my funds were low, she agreed to bet only nickels and dimes. But she was as serious as if we were playing for high stakes. While we played each hand, she concentrated on winning, but also on passing along to me words of advice about cards, as well as about life. I was rather cavalier in my attitude about gin, but fortunately had a natural card sense that made us evenly matched by the end of the summer.

The unwritten rule was that each time I lost a hand I had to reveal to Sophie a juicy tidbit about my social life, especially my dating escapades. Sophie was easy to talk to, and I found myself telling all. Sophie didn't seem to tire of hearing about my life, no matter how far removed my teen concerns must have been from her exciting, show business life that took her traveling around the world throughout the winter months.

I would drive the two of us to the club. Sophie wore a long beach robe over her bathing suit, which she matched with the turban wrapped around her blonde hair. We sat beside the pool and played gin, trying our best to ignore the stares of club members, some of whom pretended to stop to greet me but obviously were trying to get a close-up look at Sophie.

Sophie handled her fans graciously, never refusing a requested autograph, which she delivered in her bold sweeping handwriting. When word went around during her first visit there that Sophie Tucker was at the pool, crowds began gathering.

At two in the afternoon, my father came off of the golf course and saw the mob scene around the pool. He whisked us away. Sophie exited with grace and aplomb, nodding as she left on my father's arm, without making direct eye contact with the oglers.

Sophie made sure that I took our score pad with me. She planned to finish our game in the club house, where my father arranged for a private room upstairs so that we could eat lunch privately, and where we could continue our marathon gin game.

There was piped in music playing over the loud speaker. As we tallied the score, I hummed to a Frank Sinatra tune.

"You like Frankie?" Sophie asked.

I nodded. "I have most of his albums. I think he's great," I replied.

Sophie put her hand on mine. "I'll tell you something, honey. I knew Frankie when he was a kid starting out. One day I literally picked him up out of the gutter. He was stinkin' drunk. I had my driver put him in my

car. I took him to my place and sobered him up. He was a punk…drank
too much…and out of control in those days."

"Really?" I said. "Do you ever see him now?"

"In passing. He's a big shot now, but I remember…"

Sophie came by her passion for gambling naturally. Her Papa was an
inveterate gambler. The biggest worry for the family when Sophie was a
child was the card games that went on in the big room on the top floor in
Hartford. There was nothing in that room but an old round kitchen table
that had green pool-table cloth tacked over the top and a lot of battered
chairs. Papa wouldn't let any of the family into that room, but they also
couldn't get him out of it so long as a game was going on. The pinochle ses-
sions would run for hours. One game ran steadily for four days and nights.
Poker games usually started on Saturdays and would last through until
Monday or, if some players with real money came along, until Tuesday.

"Poor as we were," Sophie told me as she shuffled the cards. She was
trying to teach me how to shuffle them straight, then bend back the pack
and let them fall into place with another shuffle, something I perfected
that summer. Sophie continued, "Poor as we were, Mama always managed
to have something to give away to the ones who were worse off than we
were. If Papa had not gambled away the earnings from their restaurant,
Mama would have had more to give to the needy. Ah…""she sighed.
"Poker games! Poker once cleaned me out just the way it cleaned out poor
Pa time and time again. I couldn't buy new gowns for my act and diamonds and play poker without going broke. Yeah," she admitted. "I'm a
gambler like Pa. I even like betting on horses. Yeah, I got it from Pa.
Whenever I could in those early years, I'd run up to Hartford for a few
hours with Ma and Pa. I tried to be with them for the High Holidays,
knowing how much it meant to them to have all their family with them. I
knew Ma boasted to her buddies about "mein Sophie" who was the headliner and made so much money but always came home for the holidays.
And good ol' Pa would be doing the same to the pinochle players upstairs
and later in the back room of the saloon down in our old neighborhood

that he used to go to every day after I bought them a house. By then they sold the restaurant and lived on money I could send to them."

Sophie dealt the cards. I said very little, intent on listening to what she had to say, glimpsing the fact that Sophie had lived in many worlds that now lived in her, familiar and kaleidoscopic, her mind a play of scenes.

"Yeah, even when I was on a hectic schedule I'd stay in the theater until I finished my act in the night show, around eleven, then out for some supper and perhaps a poker game. And back to bed by three in the morning. Many times…during my burlesque days…the boys and I (the Five Kings) lived at the same hotels on the road, and after the show we six would get together and play poker. No high stakes. I usually got trimmed anyway. One thing I made clear to those guys right from the start…no drinking." Sophie took a sip of her iced tea.

"Gin!" Sophie said, throwing down her cards. "Add it up."

I did, hoping she would keep talking. I loved listening to Sophie's stories.

Sensing my interest, Sophie kept talking. "When I lived in Hollywood and was making a picture," she said, "L.B. Mayer, from MGM Studios, often invited me over to his home for Sunday brunch, served out on his patio in front of the swimming pool. Kind of like the pool at Vernon Hills only bigger and more private. There would be twenty to thirty people…everybody of any importance in film land. The food was the best I have ever eaten anywhere…always finnan haddie, a favorite dish of L.B.'s among other things. After brunch he would have a concert and then pinochle and bridge games. L.B. was a champ at pinochle, and how he loved to beat everybody he played with, which he usually did. He took me on a few times, but he was too good for me. One night, my older brother Phil, *alav ha'shalom*, was still alive, and managing my money. I lost $12,000 to L.B., and I had to telephone Phil and have him wire me the money. After that Phil got me to promise to send him every dollar I could save from my salary for him to invest and look after, so I would be sure to have a few dollars for a rainy day. Phil knew that I took after Pa in loving to gamble. Living the kind of life I lived, here, there, and everywhere, with always the temptation to get into poker games or play the horses, I would have been in the same spot that a lot of performers were but for Phil keeping me to that promise all through the years. Oh, I've broken it time and time again, and I'm always sorry. I used to get furious at Phil, *alav ha'shalom*, for budgeting me and keeping me to that budget, but even when my temper was hottest I knew deep down inside myself that he was right, and that I was a fool if I didn't pay attention to what he said."

"Do you ever plan to retire, Sophie?" I asked.

I could tell that she'd never been asked such a question, so ordinary and even domestic, nor once considered what it suggested.

"I don't know," she answered, getting pensive. "Most people live like this," she said. She drew a level line with her hand. "Some people live like this." She drew a higher line. "Having an open mind makes part of the difference. Risk makes the rest."

"Gin!" I said.

"I was just about to knock," Sophie complained. "You got me talking, and I let down my guard!" Sophie's smile was wide. "See? You do have an open mind, just like me, though not because we're blood kin. Freedom is relative. So is happiness and reality and risk. Sometimes, in order to be free, we have to take risks. Sometimes, in order to be happy, we have to take risks. As for what's real and what isn't, it's like beauty, in the eye of the beholder. Reality is one thing for one person, and another for another. We make our reality. It can be what we want, or what we need. I'm an optimist. Deep down inside, past that old inbred cautiousness that my brother Phillip had, I believe in possibility. It doesn't always matter if a thing is real. If the possibility is, that's what counts."

I studied Sophie, trying to see the brash and successful woman, whose face was on record album covers. But there were no traces of that woman here. This woman was more beautiful. She had wonder in her eyes. This was a woman who loved me enough to believe in my fantasies and wade through my doubts.

As if reading my mind, Sophie said, "Lois, you have a very special place in my heart, my dear."

I thought about what that special place must look like in her heart. I sat picturing the spot, where I could smell the sweet air of freedom. It seemed to me that all that remained was a world of possibility, one so large and bounteous that I couldn't have explored it all in an hour, a day, a year. The idea that anything in the world was possible gave me a certain freedom, which made me feel a certain power. Suddenly the power was mine, the freedom, the possibility. All these were my reality when I was with Sophie. It was a reality I could live with.

# CHAPTER 8

▼

# FAMILY REUNION

*War clouds grayed the American sky, the pace quickened and jazz came. Ragtime had given place to a new kind of music called jazz. It was made to order for Sophie. When Sophie found that she paired sizzlingly with a small hot combo, she formed Sophie Tucker's Five Kings of Syncopation, with herself as "The Queen of Jazz." She became the Queen of Jazz accompanied by the Five Kings of Syncopation. The Kings included, variously, cornetist Mannie Klein, drummer Danny Alvin and violinist Richard Himber.*

*For the next five years, Queen Soph reigned at Reisenweber's, the most famous hot spot on Broadway during the Jazz Age, intermittently leaving her domain to headline in big-time vaudeville, and taking time out for a third honeymoon. In her long career, Sophie had sung perhaps a thousand different songs. "Happy In Love" was not one of them. Her third marriage to Al Lackey also ended in divorce. And friction developed, and the Queen dismissed her Kings in 1921 after four successful years.*

Neither Sophie nor my father had forgotten about the family reunion that they had discussed several years earlier. They had both done some hard research, and come up with a guest list of those family members who were related to both of them. Their plan involved the use of our house and a big party, ostensibly so that distant relatives could come and meet Sophie Tucker, actually, however, so that Sophie could mend the rift between little Sophie and her brother little Uncle Charlie, a rift over fifty years old. No one was able to recall the exact cause of the dispute that had severed their communication; however, each person invited to the party recalled that both little Sophie and little Uncle Charlie were extremely stubborn. Sophie was haunted by the idea that these two siblings were estranged. After all, Sophie said, they were the two surviving senior family members, one from upstate New York and the other from Connecticut.

Little Sophie had a son named Irving Shaw, my father's first cousin. My father and Irving had stayed in touch over the years, and Irving promised to bring his mother to the party. Irving's wife and two daughters, Janet and Linda, were also coming.

Big Sophie (Sophie Tucker) was sure she could pull this thing off and patch up the family feud. We distinguished between Sophie Tucker and little old Aunt Sophie by calling Sophie Tucker "Big Sophie" and Aunt Sophie "little Sophie." And, indeed, she was little, under five feet tall with tiny hands and feet.

When the day of the party arrived, my mother and father hired a caterer and our living room and dining room, as well as the sun porch and patio, were filled with round tables covered with white cloths and fancy linen napkins. Flowers were everywhere. Sophie and Moe arrived hours early to help supervise the preparations. Judith flew in from college for the party. She and I helped with the preparations.

The first ones to arrive came with little kids, bratty ones whose fat mothers kept urging them to sing for Sophie. That group accompanied little Uncle Charlie and an assorted crowd of relatives from the northeastern part of the country. Sophie was gracious but clearly she was on edge, watching the door for the entrance of little Sophie. Little Uncle Charlie looked like a female version of Little Sophie, with the same tiny hands and feet, and standing less than five feet tall.

A half-hour later Irving Shaw and his wife and two daughters arrived with Little Sophie. Little Uncle Charlie and Little Sophie gaped at each other through their identical wire rimmed bifocals. Immediately, they ran towards each other and embraced. Both began to cry and hold on to each other as they fell into each other's arms. Throughout the remainder of the party they were inseparable. Big Sophie was surprised that all it took was for the two of them…brother and sister…to be in the same room, for the years of bitterness and pride to melt away. Big Sophie was pleased.

Sis (Annie) arrived next with Jules. Judith ran to them and the three of them embraced. Annie looked nothing like Sophie unless you looked closely. Annie had mousy brown hair, soft brown eyes and a slim petite figure. She wore glasses. She had the softest, kindest face I had ever seen. She and Sophie kissed and hugged. Moe joined them, wiping the perspiration from his face as he gave his little Sis Annie a wet kiss.

Daddy's sisters, Charlotte and Rose, and their families arrived, and my father proudly walked around from table to table, introducing them to the others. Janet Shaw and I were told that we looked alike. We both grinned. I didn't see the resemblance. Her sister Linda had her arm in a plaster cast; she had broken her arm in a horseback riding accident, she said. The three of us started our own table. Judith's now fiancé, Joel arrived and they stayed to themselves, sitting off in a corner balancing their plates on their laps.

People served themselves from the plentiful buffet my mother had arranged on a long table, then sat in small groups on chairs placed at the round tables. My mother was doing her best to be sociable that evening, talking about whatever matter she thought might interest people.

I took some photographs during the party, wanting to memorialize this family extravaganza. There must have been thirty-five to forty people stuffed into our house, a house that suddenly seemed too small for this large boisterous crowd of people. At one point in the evening, my mother rolled her eyes at me. The noise level had escalated. In one corner of the living room a bratty little boy around seven years old was standing on one of the wing-backed chairs, wearing his shoes, and belting out songs at Big Sophie, who shrugged her shoulders at my father. Next to this kid was a large woman urging him to sing louder and to smile.

In another section of the room, not far from where Judith and Joel were smooching, little Uncle Charlie and little Sophie were holding hands, tears streaming from their eyes. They would turn to each other and start talking simultaneously every few minutes.

Annie and Jules were talking to the Shaw family at a center table. Aunt Charlotte and Aunt Rose and their families were outside on the patio. In the sun porch sat a group of awkward pre-teens and an obese couple, distant cousins. I walked around snapping photographs. (See photographs in back section.)

Son, a.k.a. Charles, sat with Blanche to make sure she was taken care of while Moe went around to each table, playing host. My father was beaming with pride. He was proud of his house, he was warmed by the presence of family members, many of whom he hadn't seen in twenty years, and, most of all, he seemed to feel special because Sophie Tucker had chosen to hold court right here, in our home.

Sophie and Daddy came together in front of the fireplace and clapped their hands for attention.

"Attention!" Daddy yelled, but the noise level only escalated.

"Let me handle this, Milt," Sophie said, placing a hand on my father's arm. Daddy was clearly annoyed because he had been ignored.

Sophie didn't raise her voice; she simply inhaled and brought herself to her full height. In a normal tone she said, "Family, may we have your attention, please."

Immediately, the room was quiet. Those on the patio or in the sun porch also stopped talking and took places around the perimeter of the living room.

"How did you do that, Soph?" my father said, getting a big laugh from the crowd.

Sophie took the opportunity to ham it up, giving an exaggerated shrug of her shoulders and booming, "Maybe I'm better looking than you are."

Everyone shrieked with delight and clapped their hands. With such encouragement, I thought the two of them were going to launch into a burlesque routine. Actually, for a while the two bantered back and forth. I suspected that my father was in seventh heaven, enjoying the closest he'd ever come to being in show business.

When their banter stopped, the room was still as everyone waited to see what was next. Daddy turned to Sophie. "Well, Soph," he said, "it's clear that they want to hear you, not me...so how about you take it from here?" He feigned a hurt expression.

Sophie was in top form. "Milt," she said in her best stage voice, "are you surprised? Did you really dare think that the family's main draw today was to see you?" She put her hands on her hips, turned her back to Daddy, and gave the audience a look that said, "Can you believe this guy?"

The crowd loved it. They roared with laughter, stamped their feet and clapped their hands.

"Come up here, Moe," Sophie boomed at Brother. "Come on, don't be shy." Then she turned to the crowd and gave them a look that said, "Shy? Look at him; he's anything but shy."

As Moe came up and stood with his arms around Daddy and Sophie, the room rocked with more laughter. Sophie disentangled her arms from the two men and took a subtle step to the side.

"This all started because of these two guys," Sophie began. And she told the guests how Moe had gone to my father for tax advice, and how Daddy had revealed that they were cousins, and on and on, making it more dramatic and comical than it probably had been in actuality. Sophie knew how to work a crowd, even a crowd of relatives, some of whom clearly annoyed her, especially the ones who couldn't control their kids who most of the evening were tearing through the house or standing on the furniture with their shoes on.

Daddy and Moe lit two cigars, and mugged to the crowd while Sophie's spiel went on and on. The three of them were sensational together, very entertaining, and, at times, hysterically funny. And the best part was that they were ad libbing, the three of them.

They brought little Uncle Charlie and little Sophie up to the front, and Sophie made them promise that they would stay in touch and spend the rest of their lives as brother and sister and forget the nonsense that had once severed their relationship. Did they have a choice? They both promised.

In small groups, stragglers threatened not to leave; the party broke up around midnight. Sophie steered people toward the front door when they came up to have a private word with her, winking at my mother, and helping to bring the evening to a close.

By one in the morning, most everyone had departed; it was my parents, Judith and Joel, Sophie, Moe, Blanche, Charles and I. We collapsed onto various chairs. Sophie took her usual chair by the fireplace, my father the wooden rocker a few feet away. My mother and Blanche shared the small settee, while Moe chose a chair somewhat off to the side. I pulled out the piano stool and sat by the window. We said, "Whew," intermittently. My mother supervised the caterers as they cleaned up.

"We did it!" Sophie boomed. "I'm not sure I'll be up to doing it again for another twenty years."

"That's what she said to her last husband," Moe said, laughing at his own joke.

Sophie frowned at him. "Big shot. You think you're a headliner since you and Milt did your little schtick with me tonight." Then she smiled and planted a wet kiss on Moe's forehead.

"Loey," my father said. "Come on. Get out the sheet music." He pulled out the piano bench and motioned for me to sit down at the keyboard.

As tired as we were, Sophie, Moe, my mother, and I sang old show tunes around the piano. Blanche and Charles watched, grinning with exhaustion.

"Take it, Sis," Moe said, pushing Sophie.

"Loey, you think you can play my song by ear?" Sophie asked.

I knew what she wanted, and launched into a choppy rendition of *Some of These Days* on the piano while Sophie sang her theme song.

It was the perfect end to a long anticipated evening. When Moe, Sophie, Blanche and Charles piled into their waiting limousine and headed back to New York City, my parents and I went up to bed. I heard Judith come in a half-hour later and fell asleep.

# CHAPTER 9

▼

# THE DINNER PARTY

*A single again, the headliner was without accompanist. Sophie interviewed a tall, thin, bespectacled youth with somber mien and fine references. He had trouble, though, transposing and adjusting to Sophie's impromptu program changes. One Celebrity Night at Reisenweber's, he filled in for the other acts and, with no rehearsal, delivered as expertly as each unit's own man. Sophie then used him at two New York theaters. He asked if she was satisfied with his playing.*

*"I'll let you know later," she told him. Forty-five years and thousands of performances with Ted Shapiro later, she still hadn't. Flawless technique, a photographic musical memory and unfaltering taste allowed Shapiro to translate anything he once heard into an unobtrusive, colorfully matching background, be it ballad, blues or just blue. By some miracle, "The Mary Garden of Ragtime," as she had once been tagged, had lassoed the Gerald Moore of popular song. Their almost half century together would become a glowing testimonial surely without equal in the realm of music.*

Sophie insisted on throwing a dinner party for my immediate family in honor of my going away to college. It was to take place at her Park Avenue apartment. As if to affix the image in my mind to savor when I was away at college, that evening I paid particular attention to Sophie's home. It was an old apartment with high ceilings. There was a fireplace in Sophie's corner study/office and one in the living room. Rooms branched off of the Old World entry hall. To the left of the foyer was the living room whose far right wall held the elegant piano. Comfortable chairs and a small couch flanked the living room fireplace. To the right of the foyer, opposite the living room, was the dining room where we sat down to an elegantly set table dominated by heavy, gold-dipped silverware. In 1954, Sophie's sterling silver flatware had been dipped in gold to commemorate Sophie's Golden Jubilee...fifty years in show business. Every day Sophie filled an elegant silver bowl with fresh fruit and nuts and placed it in the center of the dining room table.

The dining room was rectangular, most of the space taken up by a long highly polished table. This evening, Sophie sat at one end of the table and Moe at the other. I sat at Sophie's left next to Judith. Blanche and Charles sat opposite me. My parents sat at Moe's end of the table. My back was to the windows that overlooked Park Avenue. Flowered bone china plates, linen cloth and napkins, crystal ware and a lovely floral centerpiece topped off the elegant place settings. Our utensils were golden forks, knives and spoons. It was a bright table, if somewhat palatial in appearance.

My father picked up a gold-dipped fork and examined it.

Sophie watched him. "Lady Michelham, I called her Cupie, of London once invited me to a luncheon she gave for Madame Cecile Sorel. Lord Allington and Harry Melville picked me up to take me there. When I saw the solid gold service on Cupie's table, my heart just about stopped. Sis was with me on that trip. Sis gave me a look, and I gave her one back. I whispered to Sis in Yiddish to watch Lady Michelham, and do what she did. That day I promised myself that one day I would have my silver flatware dipped in gold...and in 1954 my Golden Jubilee seemed the perfect time."

Moe motioned the maid to his side and whispered something to her. She came back with a pitcher of red wine and a glass bowl of ice cubes, which she placed beside Moe's plate. Using his bare hands, Moe scooped up two ice cubes and put them into his wine. My father grimaced.

As if on signal, Sophie raised her wineglass. "A toast to the whole mishpucha and to our Lois who is going out into the world by way of Pennsylvania. Why, I don't know." She chuckled to soften her skepticism. On the one hand, Sophie made it clear that she wanted me to remain in New York City and to attend NYU or Columbia. On the other hand, given her own early break from home, Sophie understood and cheered my decision to attend Penn State.

I was aware suddenly of Sophie squirming around with her foot under her chair. She twisted and contorted her body, shifting from one foot to the other.

"Are you okay?" I whispered to her.

"This goddamn button. I can never find it when I need it," she whispered back to me.

I nodded as if I understood, but at first I did not. Then I realized that she was banging her foot against the rug in order to locate the floor button that rang for the help to come serve the first course of our dinner.

Moe set down his wineglass and laughed. "Sis, forget it. You've never been able to gracefully buzz for dinner service. That goddamn button is a menace. One day you're going to wrench your back trying to buzz for Meesa."

"I'll do it, Brother," Sophie insisted glaring at him. "You take care of pouring more wine for Milton, and I'll handle this goddamn floor buzzer." She stamped about wildly until, at last, Meesa and a butler bearing silver food trays appeared at the dining room entranceway.

"We heard you ring for us," said the tuxedoed man.

Sophie grinned at me as if we were co-conspirators in the game of find the buzzer.

The meal was delicious: a standing rib roast, small potatoes, string beans, a tossed salad, more wine and a rich gooey dessert. Moe watched as we filled our plates and the servants offered their wares around the table, by-passing Moe without hesitation. When everyone else was served, Moe whispered something to the butler.

I was about to learn about Moe's food idiosyncrasies. He was a finicky eater. More than that, he only ate burned food...black toast, beef blackened and overdone...no exceptions. Sophie paid Moe no mind. Her household staff was familiar with Moe's eating patterns and when everyone else was served they left, only to return a few minutes later with Moe's plate, which contained burned toast, hard black flank steak, and an overdone baked potato. The plate was placed before Moe.

Blanche said little. Charles treated his mother like an invalid during dinner. He was now twenty-five years old, still stood ramrod straight, and sported a blonde crew cut. I had a glimpse that evening of the intelligent, witty, warm guy hidden beneath Charles's rather formal manner. He still treated Sophie and Moe like they were his parents.

Charles treated Blanche as if she were his dowager grandmother, rather than his mother. Blanche was wearing an auburn wig this night. Her cheeks were dotted with two splotches of red rouge. She wore a matronly dark rayon dress and heavy expensive jewelry. She smelled of heavy perfume and medicine. She clutched a white handkerchief in one hand, and her ample bosom revealed a cleavage and the white lace edging of a second emergency hanky. She mopped her face with one or the other handkerchief throughout the meal. When she spoke, which was not often, she sought Moe's approving eyes. Most of the time, however, she said nothing.

Charles and Moe appeared to have a solid father-son relationship, which included slaps on the back and mutual glances and admiring comments when a good-looking woman crossed their path.

In between the main course and dessert, small bowls filled with different colored liquid were placed at each setting. Just as Judith was about to taste her colored liquid, Sophie interrupted her with a roaring laugh which shook one end of the table. "That's a finger bowl, honey," she said to Judith. "The water is dyed different colors. Here, watch me." Sophie dipped her fingertips into the green water in her bowl and wiped them dry on her linen napkin.

We all followed Sophie's example. The staff removed the finger bowls and replaced them with our dessert plates. The rich gooey dessert was delicious.

Sophie took out her cigarettes and placed them on the table. She offered me one. I accepted. My father held a light to Sophie's Parliament cigarette, and then he and my mother each lit a cigarette.

"One time I made a real faux pas," Sophie said. "I was in London...one of my favorite places in the world. I was invited to dinner at some fancy mansion. Right before dessert was served I lit a cigarette. I noticed that everyone was frowning at me. I learned that night that the English custom is no cigarettes until the meal is over, which is signaled by a toast to the King of England."

We all laughed.

Throughout dinner Moe kept the conversation centered on Sophie, forever returning her to one place or another from her travels, so that during the course of the dinner, Sophie had described everything from the queen of England to the tiny Danish village beloved by Christian Anderson.

After dinner Sophie led us into the living room where she took her place on a small velvet winged-back chair beside the fireplace. Moe sank into the cushiony sofa, puffing on his ever-present cigar. Sophie smoked cigarette after cigarette.

Just as we were settling in, Charles stood and took his mother's hand. "I'm going to take Mother home for an early bedtime," he announced.

Blanche and Sophie touched cheeks in farewell. Sophie grabbed Charles and gave him a big hug and a wet kiss. Moe walked his wife and son to the door and then returned to his place on the couch.

Sophie turned to the rest of us. "I need some advice. I'm supposed to appear on the Ed Sullivan Show in a week, and I must decide what to wear."

On cue, Meesa entered the room with a white sequined gown over her arm.

"Meesa, hold up the dress so they can have a good look, dear," Sophie said. Sophie turned to us. "Ed says the television cameras go wacky and reflect awful beams if the glitter is too much. I had my tailor tone the glitter down a bit. What do you think?"

It was a typical Sophie Tucker trademark, so unlike Sophie's everyday street clothes. I thought about Sophie on the Ed Sullivan Show in the dress before me, leaning on Ted Shapiro's piano and waving her signature long silk scarf around as she belted out her songs and bantered with the audience.

"Loey, what do you think? You look like you have an opinion," Sophie said, interrupting my thoughts.

"It's wonderful," I said. "It will be perfect."

Sophie turned to my father.

"She's right, Soph. It's you," he said.

"Marion?" Sophie asked my mother.

"It will look lovely on you," my mother said.

Before being asked, Judith agreed. Judith was looking at three framed photographs on Sophie's mantel.

"You know, Judith," Sophie said, noticing what had captured my sister's attention. "In the hard days when I was starting out, I saved up and splurged on those three fancy frames for Mama's Papa's, and Son's photographs. These went with me everywhere. The minute I opened my grip, the photographs went on my dressing table."

Sophie stood up and took the white dress from Meesa. "Excuse me, folks," she said to us. "I'll be right back."

While Sophie was gone, my father walked over to the white marble mantel and glanced at the gold antique clock sitting on top of it. He checked his watch against it. I walked around, examining the heavily framed paintings hanging on the walls. The ambience of the room worked and reflected Sophie's world tours, china figurine collection and small photographs scattered about depicting Sophie and her friends taken during her various American and world tours.

Sophie returned. I had expected her to be modeling the Ed Sullivan dress, but here she was in a flowered bathrobe and terry cloth slippers, carrying a cigarette in one hand a cup of hot tea in the other.

"Well, Lois," Sophie began, winking at me. "I hope you're looking forward to another day with Andre'. You'll come the night before again, sleep over, and we'll get to his salon at our usual five forty-five in the morning. This time we'll lunch out, and I'll show you off, newly coifed and a real knock out. We'll have a grand time."

I touched my hair. "Has it grown that much?" I said.

"Certainly. We want Andre' to cut your hair before you leave for college. I don't want you getting it chopped up in some little college barbershop. Andre' will give you a cut that will last throughout the term."

Then Sophie turned to Judith. "And you, young lady. Soon you will be a bride. Now don't take any crap from Joel. You must set the rules early on or else you'll become a house slave."

Judith looked uncomfortable.

"I'm not trying to embarrass you or butt in, dear," Sophie added, trying to soften her words.

"That's okay," Judith said. "Don't worry about me. Joel and I love each other."

"Love, love, love. I know all about it," Sophie said.

"Now, Sophie," my father said. And he quickly changed the subject back to my haircut. "You and Lois had better select a date for your day on the town. Lois is on a tight schedule before she leaves for college."

Sophie and I selected a date before we left. Sophie walked us to the door. Just as she opened the door to let us out, a young man in a gray suit entered from the hallway, an overcoat over one arm.

Sophie offered her cheek to him and grabbed my father's arm. "Milton, you remember Bert," she said.

My father looked wary as he shook hands with Bert who was nervously pushing his way inside.

"You'll be okay, Soph?" my father said before he closed the door behind him.

"Of course, I didn't expect Son tonight, but…" and Sophie lowered her voice once Bert was inside and out of sight and added, "Writing him a check won't take long. Don't worry, Milt. I'll be in bed and asleep within the hour."

On the drive back to Mount Vernon I asked my father about Bert. "I never met Bert before," I said. "How come he's never at our family dinners?"

"He's trouble, that's why. It's a long story," my father said. "Sophie feels guilty about something from years ago when she left him in Hartford. And Bert is good at keeping her guilt afire long enough to get money out of her."

CHAPTER 10

▼

# SON AND SHOW BUSINESS

*Like good wine, Sophie improved with age. With Ted Shapiro at the piano, she became not only the last of the red-hot mammas but also the last of the great vaudevillians. The years that followed found her name in lights on the marquees of vaudeville and musical comedy theaters, motion picture palaces and gilded cafes all over the United States, in Great Britain and on the continent. She had her share of disappointments. When her talents were given full play, she was invariably successful; where she encountered incompetent interference, as in her first movie venture, the results were sometimes disastrous.*

*But with her remarkable capacity for bouncing back, Sophie Tucker followed every failure with more than compensating success. When vaudeville moved back to where it started, the cafe, Sophie Tucker became the greatest café headliner of all times, the one who week after week drew the biggest crowds from a legion of fans and friends. There has never been a more beloved entertainer.*

A week later, Sophie and I repeated my sleep-over at her apartment, up the next morning at five and off to Andre'. Afterwards we went to the Plaza for lunch.

While we ate we talked. Sophie told me that she had given her Mama her solemn promise that never, as long as she lived, would anybody else in their family go into show business. Sophie's being in it was enough for Mama.

"So, Loey," Sophie suddenly said. "You finally got to meet Bert."

I nodded.

"Bert and I have had a rocky relationship," she added.

I sat back in my chair, knowing that Sophie was about to explain.

"My mother wished better for me than her own life of domestic toil, and her advice was traditional. 'After you are through school,' she told me, 'then you must look around for a good, steady young man and get married.' In no time at all I did find a man to marry, a handsome neighbor, Louis Tuck, a beer-wagon trucker who made me feel like the belle of the ball. A week after my high school graduation, we eloped, although Mama insisted on an Orthodox wedding when we returned. I became pregnant almost immediately. When my son, Bert, was born, we moved in with my folks, and I found myself back in the restaurant kitchen, chopping vegetables and washing dishes.

"Tuck left me when I insisted he work harder to support us. I ran off to New York to try my luck as a singer, leaving Bert with my folks. I left Bert, and some condemn me for it. But no one condemns me more than I do. I have terrible pangs of guilt about it.

"When I returned for my first visit after two years away, my mother's hair had turned white and Bert barely recognized me. Bert called my sister Annie 'Mama.' Though my family forgave me, the neighbors didn't. They said only a bad woman would do such a thing. I felt like a bad woman…a whore. Because I had gone on the stage and left my child, I was considered 'no good.' I vowed not to return to Hartford until I had become a star, and stayed away for about five years. Well…after I became famous, my mother's friends made peace with my apostasy in leaving home. The one with whom I might never make peace, however, is Bert. We don't talk about my leaving him, but I have a hunch that he feels I owe him something, that the world owes him something because of it." Sophie wiped her eyes.

"When I first left him in Hartford, I sent money home weekly to support him, and later to pay tuition so that he could go away to military school. Whenever Son had a vacation from boarding school, either Mama or Sister would bring him to New York to see me. I remember one visit when I took Son out for dinner and he had his first taste of oysters. Oysters were forbidden in his grandparents' kosher home, and it was the first time Bert had ever seen them.

"Never will I forget," she said, tears of laughter on her face. "We had oysters, all right...big ones. I had to gulp to get mine down. We were with Al...Al Lackey...my husband at the time. Son tried to eat an oyster, but failed, and had to pull the oyster out of his throat with his fingers. Perhaps he felt everybody watching him; anyway, he flopped the oyster down on his plate in frustration, took his knife and cut the oyster in two. He ate the pieces with a fork. It was his first and last experience with oysters."

I knew that Sophie was on a roll...remembering the past, and reviewing Bert's part in that past. She continued. "One night when I was playing my burlesque club, the Playground, I got the shock of my life. Eddie Cantor and George Jessel showed up for an evening of fun. I had just helped Eddie at a benefit, so he owed me a favor. There was a big crowd that night. Eddie and Georgie were the masters of ceremony. I was busy hopping from table to table, meeting customers. I looked up when I heard Eddie making an announcement. 'Now, ladies and gentlemen,' he said, 'we are going to introduce a young fellow...a dancer. This is his first appearance in public. His mother is a very well known performer, but he asked me not to mention her name. He wants to make it on his own. After he dances, and if you like him, I'll tell you who he is'

"At that moment I was called into my office. When I came out I stood at the rear of the club and saw a kid out on the floor dancing a mile a minute. 'Gee,' I said aloud, 'he looks a lot like Son.' I moved up closer to the dance floor. 'My God, it's my Son!' I yelled. 'Eddie! Georgie! Bert! What are you doing here?' By now the place was in an uproar. I heard the crowd yelling, 'It's Sophie's son. Isn't he a fine looking boy? A good dancer, too.' Then there was thunderous applause. I was stunned. I had no idea that Son danced or knew anything about show business. He had been in military school since he was six years old. He was then about fifteen. I had never permitted him to hang around the theater or club where I was working. Because of Mama I had been against his going into show business. I had told him many times when he'd say he wanted to be an actor that as long as his grandmother was alive it was out of the question. Now here was Son, dancing his heart out. I was pleased that Son had put it over and I couldn't help admitting he danced well. But, when we got home, I laid the law down to him. 'No show business for you until you finish your education,' I told him. After a while I did soften up and promised to send him to a dancing school to learn some routines. I also promised that at the proper time I would groom him and set him sailing on the ocean of show business if his heart was still on it when that time came." Sophie took a sip of her water and sighed deeply.

"Go on," I said, interested in learning as much as I could about Sophie's relationship with Bert. Maybe I was threatened by the idea that Sophie had a child of her own, albeit a grown son. I enjoyed the attention she gave me. Somehow, I believed that the more I understood her relationship with Bert, the less threatened I would feel. So I urged Sophie to continue.

She did. "Another time in Rufus Le Maire's show 'Le Maire's Affairs,' Rufus gave Bert a job in the show. Son carried one of the signs in the minstrel parade, up and down the aisle and onto the stage. Everybody back stage used to kid Bert. They tried out all the old show business pranks on him, even sent him out to different theaters to find the key to the curtain, until Bert got wise to them.

"When Son was scheduled to appear at the Oriental, I called up my friend Leslie to go with me to catch Son's act. There was no publicity about it. Son had told Paul Ash not to introduce him as Sophie Tucker's son because he wanted to make good on his own.

"I wore dark glasses to the theater. When the show started after the movie, I began to get the jitters. Every time Paul Ash introduced a kid, my heart jumped up into my throat. Paul had a bunch of clever youngsters, Ginger Rogers, Milton Watson, Sy Landry, Johnny Perkins. After two or three acts, it was Son's turn. When he came on stage I slid down in my seat, more scared than I had ever been in any theater. I grabbed hold of Leslie's hand. I was worried that Son would make his entrance as a know-it-all, fresh kid, but he didn't. He came on smiling, quiet, like a little gentleman. He walked over to Paul Ash, shook his hand and thanked him like a gentleman. Then Son faced the audience and started his introductory number and soft-shoe dance. It went over well. He accepted the applause just the way I would have had him to.

"Suddenly Son announced, 'Now, ladies and gentlemen, I will give you my impression of that popular song, the "Turkish Towel" number, as sung by my mother, Miss Sophie Tucker.' There was a buzz of excitement throughout the theater. People turned around to try to find me, but I was so low in my seat I was practically invisible. Son waited for the audience to quiet down, then he gave his impersonation of me. The audience ate it up. I noticed that son's hands were trembling and his legs were getting shaky. He still had his big Charleston number to do. But he pulled himself together. Before I knew it, Son was into his dance, his legs flying. More applause. He was a hit. He ran off the stage. Paul Ash called him back out and complimented him. Poor Son, his legs were shaking so hard he could hardly walk. As for me, I had just about broken Leslie's arm. Then I heard Son yell, 'Ma! Where are you, Ma?'

"I flew out of my seat and ran down the aisle toward the stage. 'I'm coming, Son, I'm coming!' I screamed. I took him in my arms. The audience was cheering, but I could feel Son trembling all over.

"'Did I do all right, Ma?' he whispered. 'I'm proud of you today,' I told him. Then I turned to the audience and spoke," Sophie now had tears in her eyes.

I put my hand on hers. I wanted her to go on. She did.

"I said, 'For the fourteen years that I have been coming to Chicago you have accepted me in everything I have had the pleasure of bringing for your approval. Not once have you ever let me down. Today Sophie Tucker, the mother, gave you her son, and you accepted him, for which I am deeply grateful. May you all live to enjoy the pleasure and thrill of your children as I have today with my son.' That's what I told them," Sophie concluded.

"Then what happened?" I asked.

"Son left Le Maire's Affairs to go out on his own with a warning from me that he was primarily a dancer which meant continuous rehearsing and always getting new routines. I told him that he if did songs, new ones must continuously go in his act. I said, 'There are four or five shows daily in the theaters you're booked to play. You will need rest. You can't do any running around.' Bert was rather a wild one. 'Take care of your health, first, last, and all the time. If you pay attention to what I say now, you'll make a success of show business. If you don't, I give you less than two years, and you're finished.' I give that same advice to all the youngsters who are starting out on their own and come to me."

"Did he listen to you?" I asked.

"No he didn't, and my advice proved to be sound. Son was too pig-headed to listen to me, and too crazy wild to stop his shenanigans. For years I worried myself sick over Son. I was sure he would marry a *shicksa* one day."

"Did he?" I asked.

Sophie shook her head. "It seems as if all of our family's news was always being wired or cabled to me in those days. I was playing in Manchester, England early the summer of 1931. I was just getting ready to go on for the second show when a cable was handed to me. It said, 'I was married today to a fine Jewish girl. Love Son.' That's when I learned that Bert was married to a woman named Lillian, a *Yiddisha madela*. When Al and I sailed home from Cherbourg at the end of that summer, I had something to look forward to: the meeting with my new daughter-in-law Lillian."

"And, did you like her?" I asked.

Sophie shook her head. "Enough, enough. I've said enough. I'm getting aggravated now. All I can say is Lillian and Bert are a lot alike. They have no children and probably never will. They're always short of money, and I help them out when I can." Sophie picked up the dessert menu. "What shall we have for dessert?"

"I'm full," I said.

"Come on, we'll split something," Sophie insisted. "You won't be getting food as good as this in college." She called over the waiter and ordered apple pie a la mode with two spoons.

The following week I left for Penn State, and Sophie left on a European singing tour. She sent me a letter or postal card from each city on her tour. Whenever I checked my college mailbox, I hoped for word from Sophie. When something arrived, I read it over several times, and closed my eyes and tried to picture her. Sometimes I remembered her sweet, clean smell. When Sophie returned from Europe I was in the middle of final exams. She called one night from my parents' house.

"There's someone here who wants to say hello," my father said. I heard him hand the phone to someone.

"Loey! I miss you, darling."

"Oh, Sophie, I'm so glad to hear your voice. I got your mail, but it wasn't the same as talking to you," I said.

"And it's high time you and I had one of our heart-to-heart talks, isn't it?" Sophie said, chuckling.

"It is…it really is," I said. "When will I see you? I'll be home for winter break. Maybe we'll get together."

"If I'm in town," Sophie said. "I have a busy work schedule all winter…playing across this country, a trip to Australia…we'll have to see."

Suddenly I felt like Bert, left behind because of Sophie's career. But, I reminded myself, who the hell was I. She had a life to lead and so did I. I'd take what I could get of her time and savor every moment.

Meanwhile, I had her letters to hold me over. When I got Sophie's letters I ripped them open and read the news. Her mail came from different towns where she was appearing. Sometimes it made me think that somehow, in a strange way, there were a few strong binding strands between us. I'd picture Sophie in Europe or Las Vegas, depending on the postmark on the envelope, giving her show, then returning to her hotel room and writing to me so I could read the letters and learn something new. It seemed like it was all one big family chain without one unconnected link.

Sometimes I pretended that I was far away from the college campus, and then Sophie's deep voice came to me. Each time I received one of her letters I was happy that she hadn't changed her mind about liking me and carrying me in a special place in her heart.

Sometimes, while lying in my bed in the college dormitory I'd recall Sophie's clean, flowery smell and the sound of her words. I loved recalling Sophie's sweet smell, and thought that if I lost my sense of smell, I would have no memories.

# CHAPTER II

▼

# MOM CHUNG

*Essentially a vaudeville top liner, Sophie Tucker broke into the legitimate the-*
*ater with "Merry Mary" and "Louisiana Lou," both in 1911. "Hello,*
*Alexander" (1919) put her name on a legit marquee for the first time, and she*
*spiced up revues such as "Town Topics," "Shubet Gaietie" (1919) and "Earl*
*Carroll's Vanitie" (1924).*

  *Having attained the zenith of success in the American variety theater,*
*Sophie now looked for new worlds to conquer. She set out for London. Great*
*Britain acclaimed her even more loudly than her homeland. She became the*
*idol of the populace and the weekend guest of dukes and duchesses. She co-*
*starred with Jack Hulbert in London in "Follow A Star" (1930).*

  *New York welcomed her back warmly, but the theater world was undergo-*
*ing a change. Radio was making new popular idols. Vaudeville was losing its*
*patrons to the stage shows in the new movie palaces. Pictures were beginning to*
*talk and sing. And Sophie was approaching middle age...still handsomely*
*attractive, but no longer the flaming, youthful red-hot mama. A change in*
*style and personality was in order.*

*Her big Broadway smash was "Leave It To Me!" (1938), with William Gaxton, Victor Moore and Mary Martin. Sophie enlivened musical comedy once more with George Jessel in "High Kickers" (1941), repeated in London in 1948. Her film stints were fewer. She starred in "Honky Tonk" (1929) and had lead roles in "Broadway Melody 1937" and "Thoroughbreds Don't Cry," with Garland and Rooney (1937), and "Follow the Boys" (1944) and "Sensations of 1945."*

*The facile pen of a songwriter named Jack Yellen held the key to her middle aged change in style. Like many another vaudevillian, Sophie had sung "Down By The O-HI-O," "Lovin' Sam," "Louisville Lou," "Hard-Hearted Hannah," "Mamma Goes Where Papa Goes," and numerous other comedy hits which were Yellen's singular contribution to Tin Pan Alley. He began writing songs for Sophie's exclusive use. "I'm the Last of the Red-Hot Mammas," she proclaimed in a song by Jack Yellen which inaugurated her new personality and billing. "Life Begins At Forty," she humorously assured the middle-aged ones in her audience. The public roared for more such songs, and Yellen continued to provide them, especially tailored for Sophie, spiced with Rabelaisian humor and satirically factual in their observations on human foibles and weaknesses.*

*Of a different pattern was Yellen's "Yiddishe Momme" which marked a new epoch in Sophie's singing career. She introduced it and made it a worldwide favorite among peoples of all nationalities.*

The next time I saw Sophie was the end of my freshman year of college. I was home for a few weeks before I was accompanying my parents on a trip to California. Sophie was home from a spa on an island near Majorca. It was on that trip that she met a little Italian shoemaker who made her a pair of beautiful dressy shoes for her act, shoes that turned out to be the most comfortable she had ever tried. Sophie's hours of performing kept her on her feet a lot, and shoe comfort was one of her top priorities. She commissioned this shoemaker to make her shoes to go with every evening gown that she owned. She packed one large trunk with these new shoes and brought them home. Sophie returned home around the same time that I did from college.

The first thing Sophie showed me when my parents and I arrived at her apartment was her trunk full of new shoes. Then she told us about Mom Chung.

Mom Chung was one of Sophie's closest friends, a woman famous in her own right for providing a haven for World War II American soldiers coming home from the Eastern war zones and flying first to San Francisco. Mom Chung was usually their first choice for a home cooked meal, a comfortable home-like place to stay, and some TLC.

Mom Chung was known throughout San Francisco, and was a celebrity in San Francisco's China Town district. Sophie and Mom Chung had become close friends during World War II and had maintained that friendship right through the fifties and sixties.

Sophie wrote Mom Chung's address and telephone number on a piece of paper and gave it to my father. "Here's Mom Chung's address and number. You must call her when you get to San Francisco. I'll let her know ahead of time to expect you," Sophie said. "Before you leave and take Lois away, give me a few minutes alone with her, will you?" Sophie requested. "We'll only be a minute."

Sophie led me into her study and motioned me into a chair across from her desk.

"I've missed you," she began.

"Me, too," I said.

"You haven't forgotten your family have you?" Her eyes suddenly brightened, and she smiled, "I thought you'd forgotten me," she said.

"Of course, not, Sophie," I said.

"I hope you write to your Mom and Daddy every week and call home. Family is the most important thing in your life…don't forget that!"

"I know that," I said.

"Now, you're going to meet lots of guys at college and even on this trip you're taking with your folks. Keep your head about you. Don't be promising that Barry guy from high school anything…not yet, meet lots of fellas. Concentrate on your studies, but also have some fun. Date a lot of different fellas before you get serious. You're a good looking girl, Loey, and you'll have lots of guys interested in you."

She watched me a moment longer, and I could see that she was thinking of me in a way that no one else ever had, not merely as the girl I was, but as the woman I might someday be. She opened her desk drawer and handed me a little box with a pink bow. "I bought you a little something as a going away gift for your trip," she said. "Open it."

Inside was a blue poodle pin with a ruby eye and a little diamond collar. It reminded me of the bathroom accessories my mother had bought when she redecorated our bathroom for Sophie's first visit to our house. How long ago that now seemed.

"Do you like it?" Sophie asked.

"I love it," I said, and pinned it to my blouse. "I'll think of you whenever I wear it," I said.

"Then, darling, wear it often," she said, grinning at me. "And don't forget, take care of Cousin Janet when she gets to Penn State next year. Show her the ropes."

"Cousin Janet?"

"Haven't you heard. She was accepted at your college and will be starting in September. I'm counting on you to help her," Sophie said.

"I won't let you down," I assured her.

Before we left, Sophie gave me one of her warm soft hugs and a wet kiss on both cheeks. I think we both had tears in our eyes; I know I did.

Mom Chung met my parents and me at the San Francisco Airport. She was a small woman in wired spectacles, with a full, soft, kind Chinese face. Her smile was contagious as was her warmth and enthusiasm about meeting some of Sophie's family.

She led us to a car and driver waiting outside of the baggage area. She sat in the passenger seat next to the driver, and in Chinese directed him to drive us to our hotel.

"I wish you all had agreed to stay with me," Mom Chung said, when we arrived at the St. Francis Hotel.

"It's very nice of you to offer," my father said, "but there are three of us, and this will be easier for all of us."

"Three is nothing for me," Mom Chung said, "but I understand. During the war, however, I often had six or seven returning American GI's staying at my house. But, no matter. Sophie told me all about the three of you, and I promised her that I would take good care of you while you're visiting San Francisco."

The four of us agreed to meet that evening at Mom Chung's house at six. She insisted on sending the driver for us at five thirty.

Mom Chung's house was on Knob Hill. It was one of San Francisco's old Victorians, situated on a narrow street, a steep hilly street. Like many of the houses in the area, it was creatively painted on the exterior. The front door was massive with stained glass windows on either side. We climbed up the steep front stairs and rang the bell.

Mom Chung greeted us with warm hugs and a wide grin. "Come in, come in, my friends," she said, leading us through a second door which opened into a small hallway. She led us into a room to the left, a sitting room.

"Hello, come in," someone called from inside.

"Take it easy Sophie," Mom Chung called out.

"Sophie, Sophie, cough, cough, cough," the voice screeched.

"That's the most famous member of the household," Mom Chung quickly explained.

She turned on the parlor light and Sophie the parrot, in all her plumage and glory filled the room with coughing sounds that were a fine imitation of Sophie Tucker's smoker's cough. Mom Chung explained that her parrot was enamored of Sophie Tucker, and did a mean imitation. Whenever the parrot heard Sophie's name mentioned, she coughed like Sophie, and then, as we soon discovered, a fine imitation of Sophie's deep sexy voice singing *Some of These Days*, which she was belting out as we sat down on small Queen Anne velvet chairs.

The room was charming with World War II memorabilia on the walls and atop every end table.

"Hack, hack!" the parrot coughed and then called Sophie's name.

Mom Chung served us tea and encouraged us to browse through her many photograph albums and scrapbooks filled with the faces of soldiers on their way home from World War II. For many of them, Mom Chung explained, her house was the first civilized homestead they had been in after coming off of battlefields and ships and heading home to various towns and cities throughout the United States.

Clearly, many of the soldiers had stayed in touch with Mom Chung for many years after they stopped for a warm bed and meal in her home. In fact, she told us, a large percentage of them came back to visit her, often bringing their families, new babies, sweethearts and the like. She was godmother to many a veteran's baby or grandbaby.

One scrapbook held newspaper articles and photographs about Mom Chung and the important role she played in the lives of these many soldiers, sailors and airmen. Included in that scrapbook was a photograph of Mom Chung and Sophie Tucker. Mom Chung was cited for the role she played as "Mom" to the many soldiers stepping foot on American soil for the first time since being shipped out to war. Sophie Tucker was cited for the role she played in entertaining the troops and for her deep friendship with Mom Chung.

"Now," Mom Chung said after several hours of showing us her artifacts, "we have reservations and a private room at an authentic Chinese restaurant...a place where no tourists can be found."

That was the beginning of a whirlwind tour of San Francisco, of Mom Chung's Chinatown, of Mom Chung's world and far-reaching influence. Mom Chung's private Chinatown afforded us opportunities to meet people and see sights and taste foods that I have never again been able to duplicate.

Our last night with Mom Chung, we took her out for dinner. When a photographer came to our table, my father requested that he take our picture. (See photographic section) We kept one copy and gave one to Mom Chung to add to her photograph album.

The morning we left for New York, Mom Chung accompanied us to the airport. She gave us a shopping bag filled with assorted packages wrapped with tissue paper. "Please, give this to Sophie when you see her," Mom Chung said. "Tell her that her bedroom is all ready for her next visit, and that Sophie Parrot is asking for her all the time. Please, encourage her to come visit me." Mom Chung's eyes were moist.

My parents promised to deliver both her message and her packages to Sophie. As we boarded the airplane, I turned and waved to Mom Chung who was standing on the airfield waving her final farewell.

# CHAPTER 12

▼

# TAKE CARE OF JANET

*The beloved matriarch of the variety stages now was edging sixty, but two more overflowing decades marked her charts before she unwillingly called it a day: a world tour in 1962; three trips to Israel; joint appearances with Ted Lewis and George Jessel.*

*Sophie Tucker was the most accomplished female vocalist to come out of the ragtime tradition. When performing in a theater or cabaret, her awesome contralto voice could be heard for blocks.*

*"When I started out I had a distinctive style," she recalled. "I never sang on the beat, but slightly after it."*

*It was called an "after beat," and in those years was popularly referred to as ragtime. Tucker was famous for being the first singer to go into a fast tempo, a trick that was picked up by many of the orchestras.*

Following the California trip, I prepared to return to Penn State for another year. Sophie was away on tour, and I didn't get a chance to see her before I left for school. However, the first week that I was back at State

College, Pennsylvania, I received a note from Sophie reminding me to take care of Cousin Janet Shaw, little Aunt Sophie's grand daughter, and "teach her some of the social graces that would help her be popular with guys on campus. You know the ropes, Lois, and I'm counting on you to be Janet's mentor."

I hadn't seen Janet since the family reunion at my house in Mount Vernon. According to Sophie's next letter to me, my going to Penn State had influenced Janet's decision to go there too, a decision that Sophie had whole heartedly encouraged and supported. "Family should stick together," Sophie wrote, "so go ahead and take on this important role. Keep me posted and write to me often."

Janet was settled in the freshmen dormitory when I returned to campus. I stopped by the dorm, but she was not in her room. I taped a note to her door, welcoming her to campus and asking that she call me so that we could get together as soon as possible.

My tutelage of Janet began with a dinner out at the Bolsberg Steak House, rumored to be the best eatery in the College Park area. Janet and I were happy to be together. She didn't seem homesick or out of place, as Sophie had led me to believe. In fact, I wasn't so sure that Janet needed my help at all.

At Janet's request, I ordered dinner for both of us. As we waited for our food to be served, Janet fidgeted, tearing a small piece of paper into tiny shreds and playing with her silverware.

"I'm not real sure of myself in social situations," Janet confessed.

She suddenly looked so innocent and scared to me that I wanted to throw my arms around her and hug her to me, but I knew that would only embarrass her more. "So," I said to myself, "Once again, Sophie is right. Janet needs someone to take her under their wing."

"Don't worry, Janet. After all, we're family. Tonight is just the beginning. Lesson one is a demonstration on dinner out with a date at a place like the Bolsberg Steak House. You're a cute girl, and guys will be wanting to take you out to dinner. Pay attention, and ask me anything you think I might know...not that I'm an expert. I'm anything but!"

Janet sighed and relaxed a little. "Well, I'm not sure you're right about guys asking me out, but I'm willing to learn. Can I tell you something?" Janet leaned forward and lowered her voice.

"Sure," I said.

"I've never gone out on a date," she said, blushing as she spoke.

"So what...neither have lots of freshmen. You're starting a new stage of life now...you're a college coed. It's a new beginning. You'll have lots of dates, lots of dinners out, and lots of fun at Penn State. I promise," I said.

Janet watched me closely to see what I did with my linen napkin and which fork I used to eat my salad and then she imitated me. We were doing just fine.

The waiter brought our main course. We each had a dinner plate containing a sizzling Bolsberg Steak House steak, a baked potato and a mound of green peas.

"I'll never be able to gracefully cut my steak," Janet said, sawing away at the first piece.

"Sure you will. Watch," I said, slicing a bite-sized piece of steak from the end and keeping it on my fork. "Follow me."

Janet began to cut when her knife slipped, sending the whole steak flying across the restaurant floor, baked potato soaring through the air, and peas shooting every which way and landing on various patrons throughout the restaurant.

Janet's face turned bright red.

"Take a deep breath," I coached her. "Here, give me your empty plate, and let me take the blame for this," I insisted, trying hard not to laugh, but feeling the rise of hysterical giggles mounting in my throat. "It's okay, Janet, what the hell." And I grabbed her plate and exchanged hers for mine when I saw our waiter bounding across the room, towels in hand, a worried look on his face as he headed for our table.

"What happened here?" he asked.

Janet was near tears and stuttered something incomprehensible.

I took charge. "I'm awfully sorry, Sir," I said calmly, determined to contain my laughter. "My knife must have slipped and the rest…" I gestured outward with my hands. "May I please have another steak…in fact, a new full order…I'll pay the difference, if necessary," I said, trying to sound blasé.

The waiter nodded, removed my empty plate and also Janet's in order to keep it hot, and retreated to the kitchen. Once he was out of sight I had to release the giggles I had been suppressing. Janet caught my fever and soon she, too, was laughing.

When our new dinners arrived we started again. This time Janet sliced her steak without incident, and from there to the end of the meal, we ate like bandits, ravenous from waiting so long to eat, and relieved that we had handled the crisis so well.

Before I went to bed that night I wrote Sophie a long letter, describing the steak fiasco and exaggerating some of the details for comic affect. Sophie loved it. Her letter in response informed me that not only did she get a good laugh, but also she gained faith in her own ability to know when someone needed mentoring. Further, she said that it renewed her faith in my ability to come through in the role of mentor. And finally, she wanted me to think about a career in creative writing. My letters had proven to her that I was a talented writer, and that it was important that I start thinking about a career, and making a contribution to society either in a creative endeavor or in the field of social service.

It was the first time I seriously contemplated becoming a writer, and the idea was mildly appealing.

# CHAPTER 13

▼

# JAYNE MANSFIELD AND "THE MURDERER"

*It was well known in the Black show business community that Sophie Tucker would give Black composers a chance. After her great success with "Some of These Days," Sophie gladly featured songs by Black writers. She sang Eddie Green's "A Good Man Is Hard To Find," Spencer Williams' "Wait Until Your Papa Comes Home," and "I Ain't Got Nobody," as well as Sissie and Blake's first collaboration "It's All Your Fault." When Sophie Tucker sang a song like "After You've Gone" or "St. Louis Blues" at Reisenwebers and the Palace Theatre, the songs became hits and then standards.*

Sophie fashioned herself the last word in judging the appropriateness of a family member's spouse or intended spouse. Although Sophie was raised in an Orthodox Jewish home, she had to keep up with the times. For example, she learned to accept Blanche, who was not Jewish; and later Charles's wife Susie, also not Jewish.

Sophie believed that she could read people, that she had special intuition and could spot a charlatan a mile away. In more than a majority of cases, she was, indeed, a good judge of character.

Sophie met Joel before his and Judith's August wedding. Sophie said little the first time when Joel stopped by when Sophie was visiting our house in Mount Vernon. But after Joel left she took my sister aside and said, "Be careful, Judith. I know you think you love him, but take your time. Are you sure you want to get married in August? Why not wait a year or two? And, please, don't get pregnant right away, either. You're not pregnant already, are you?"

"Of course not," Judith answered. "I love Joel. Why don't you like him?"

"I don't trust him. He's sneaky. I don't like his eyes…they're the eyes of a murderer. I'm sorry to say so, but he does," Sophie said bluntly.

When it was clear that Judith was not taking Sophie's advice seriously and that the August wedding was going to take place as planned, Sophie didn't change her opinion, although she did make a good show about accepting Joel. She called him "the murderer" whenever she talked about Joel. Claiming that she had to be on tour in England on their wedding day, Sophie invited the wedding couple and my parents to the El Morocco Nightclub in New York City as her guests.

That night, Jayne Mansfield was the headliner at the El Morocco, doing her nightclub act with her muscle boys. Mansfield was a busty, blonde with six or seven he-men guys in bathing suits made of lion skin.

Jayne Mansfield paraded around with her big bosoms. Sophie's table was ringside. Most of the patrons at the nightclub spotted Sophie and came up to the table to get her autograph. Jayne Mansfield noticed the line of people around Sophie's table and couldn't help but spot Sophie. Sophie was used to being the center of attention. She was in her glory, but Mansfield was the headliner at El Morocco and Sophie part of the audience. Mansfield stood blocking Sophie with her back to her and shook her breasts at the remainder of the audience.

Sophie was steaming until she could no longer control herself. "How vulgar this is!" Sophie boomed at my father. Sophie had a loud voice. Obviously she wanted everyone to know she was in the audience. "Such bad taste...so vulgar!" she boomed non-stop. The person working the spotlight heard the heckles and suddenly aimed the spotlight at Sophie's table. Sophie succeeded in drawing attention and being seen.

Sophie turned to Joel and said in a loud voice, "Murderer, get me a waiter and the check." Even in the midst of her public competition with Mansfield, Sophie was unwilling to drop her nickname for Joel.

Joel lit Sophie's Parliament cigarette hoping to calm her down. She played with her flat gold cigarette case. While they waited for the waiter to bring the check, Sophie spouted off about good taste in songs.

"I've made it a rule to have a double entendre song in my act, something funny but certainly not salacious," Sophie said in her loud voice. Softer she said to Joel and Judith, "I try to start off with a lively rag, then a ballad followed by a comedy song and a novelty number. And finally the hot song. In this way, I leave the stage with the audience laughing their heads off. For encores I have popular songs, new ones. I'm determined to be different. Always was." She upped the volume. "But this...this tonight...it's simply vulgar. I've never sung a single song in my whole life to purposely shock anyone. I sing to entertain." More quietly she continued, "My hot numbers are all written around something that's real in the lives of millions of people. They're songs that mean something to everybody who hears them. One of my most popular, *Life Begins at Forty*, is a hot song, but I insist that it is not dirty. It expresses what everybody who shivers at the word middle-aged feels...the longing to make life over, to live it more fully and freely, to have more love and a lot more laughs." Then, louder, "MY hot numbers are all moral. NOT LIKE THIS CRAP! Mine have to do with sex, but not vice. And mine are all written in the first person. When I'm singing them I'm talking about myself." Softer: "The audience likes it better that way; they enjoy it when I make fun of myself in my songs. They laugh at me, at whatever predicament I find myself in. And their laughter is mixed with the knowledge that the same thing could happen to them. But tonight..." Louder: "Jayne Mansfield is vile and vulgar!"

Joel helped Sophie stand and draped her white fox stole around her shoulders. "Thank you, murderer," she said softly. And out she stormed in the middle of Mansfield's act, her mishpucha trailing after her.

# CHAPTER 14

▼

# CHRISTMAS CARDS

*Raised in an Orthodox Jewish home, Sophie abandoned a great deal of the Jewish practice with which she'd been raised when she got married without her family's knowledge or consent, and finished the process when she ran away from home to go on the stage. For the rest of her life, she had a tenuous, but deeply emotional bond to Judaism that was reciprocated and replicated by the sometimes conflicted, but likewise deeply emotional bond that the Jewish public had with her. The first time she admitted to feeling conflicted between her career and her faith was in 1920, when she was already an established headliner Yom Kippur came, and she went to shul to say Yizkor for her father, but then departed as usual for her shows, though she fasted during the holiday. It seems that for her, Judaism was a culture, a community, and only tangentially a set of actual religious practices or a system of beliefs. She could read Hebrew, but very slowly.*

*One of Sophie's greatest hits, "My Yiddische Momme," written by Jack Yellen for her, became a kind of anthem. She learned it painstakingly in transliterated Yiddish, and sang it for nearly her entire career everywhere she played.*

Sophie's address book was carefully kept. There were over five thousand names in it; each one of those people received a Christmas card from her every year. Her correspondence was extraordinarily prodigious. She would send out notes whenever she toured, letting people know she was coming to town and looked forward to seeing them. Her correspondence with critics and booking agents was noteworthy; she thanked them for every word written about her, every concession that was made for her in a new theater in terms of lighting, setting, or dressing rooms.

In early December of 1960, Sophie called me at Penn State with a request.

"Lois!" she boomed into the telephone. "It's Cuz Sophie."

"Hi, Soph," I said. "Everything okay?"

"Yes, yes, dear. When do you come home for your winter break?" she asked.

"In a week," I said. "Why?" I couldn't imagine what this call was about.

"I need your help," she said, in her usual way of making a request sound more like an order.

"What can I do?"

"It's my Christmas cards. I send out cards every year. I'm behind schedule this year, and I need you to work with me to get the damn things addressed, stamped, and into the mail. When can you come to my place?" she said.

"I leave campus next week. I could come down to your apartment a week from this Saturday."

"I'll expect you. Lois, there's no one else I can trust this to. I can always count on you, honey. See ya then," Sophie said, and before I could answer she had hung up.

When Saturday came I made it down to Sophie's apartment. Meesa greeted me at the door and led me into Sophie's dining room where Sophie sat, surrounded by envelopes, cards, stamps, endless lists of names and addresses, and a look of frustration on her face.

"Thank God, you're here. Come here, come here. Give me a kiss and sit here, beside me," she said, putting out her cigarette in the glass ashtray that was already overflowing with cigarette butts.

I kissed her soft cheek and inhaled her familiar sweet smell. "Hi, Sophie," I said.

"I'm ready to get to work."

"Okay. That's what I like to hear. I've only gotten as far as the E's, and I have to get these Christmas cards into the mail as soon as possible. I'm overwhelmed, I'm afraid," she said, throwing up her hands in desperation.

"Tell me what you want me to do, and I'll get started," I said, sitting down next to her.

I took the part of the list from the M's to the Z's after I convinced Sophie that it wasn't necessary for both of us to work from the same list at the same time in order to keep the cards in alphabetical order.

"Of course, I've been so mired down in this that I lost my perspective," she said. "But what about the cards on which I want to write a short personal note? How will I be able to get to them if they're on your list?" she asked.

"Simple," I said. "Look at the entire list and put a check mark next to the ones you want to write a note on. When I get to those I will set them aside for you to add your notes to. How about that?"

"Brilliant, brilliant!" she said, in her exuberant way.

We worked side by side for the first two hours. Wherever Sophie had penciled in a check mark next to a name, I set aside that card and envelop for Sophie to work on later. That pile soon became unwieldy, and Meesa brought us an empty carton, and we placed those awaiting her notes in the carton. Alphabetical order no longer mattered.

By the third hour, Sophie put down her pen and yawned. "I think I'll hire someone to address envelopes, stamp, seal and mail these next year," she said.

"Good idea," I said. "Have you always done these by yourself?" I asked.

"Somehow, the list has grown, and this year's list seems especially long," Sophie said. "It's time to admit that it's worth while for me to hire someone to help in the future. I get so damned pig-headed, I know. I think if I don't do it myself, they'll be done wrong. I think it's time to let go."

I laughed in agreement. "I think so, Sophie. You're so hard on yourself." The poor woman was in agony. She was rubbing her back and groaning.

"I think that's true," she said, grinning at me. "Yes, it's perfectly true. Meanwhile, I think it's too late to get anyone this year. It's almost Christmas. With your help, I think we'll do it. What do you think?"

"I'll work as fast as I can," I promised, "but I think we should get some more people to help."

"Moe's handwriting is impossible. Meesa can't do it with us. Charles…well, I don't know," she said. "Any suggestions?"

"I have an idea. Whatever we don't get done today, I'll take home and work on for the next several days at home. When they're done, I'll bring them down to you…you can add any personal notes you want, and then we'll get them over to the post office. What do you say?"

"Let them out of my sight!" Sophie was clearly threatened and scared.

"Sophie, I'll take responsibility for them. If I mess up, I'll take the blame. But I won't mess up. If I promise to do it, I'll do it. Trust me," I said, echoing her favorite admonition to me to trust her.

She immediately recognized this turn-about of roles. "All right. You win. I'm through right here and now! Let's go inside and relax. You'll take this mess back home with you." As soon as she said the words panic filled her face. "I don't know," she hesitated.

"Come on, give it up," I teased.

Sophie stood up and came toward me with outstretched hands, a smile on her face. "What would I do without you, Lois?" She kissed me on each cheek.

I looked at my watch. It was already four o'clock in the afternoon. We had been working since eight o'clock that morning…eight hours.

"Do you have plans for the evening?" Sophie asked.

I nodded.

"Well, I do too, honey," she said. "Moe is picking me up at seven. We're going out to dinner with some fans from London, and then I have a show to do. Do you have a date with a fella?"

I nodded.

"Well, come on. We have plenty to talk about."

I was ready to leave. The whole day had been very trying; addressing envelopes non-stop, sitting in one position all day in a stiff chair. I was looking forward to getting home, relaxing in a warm bubble bath, and enjoying a night on the town. "Sophie, I have to get back," I said. "I have to catch the train back to Mount Vernon. If I don't leave soon I'll be late."

"Forget the train, honey. You can't be lugging all these cards and lists over to Grand Central and onto the train. You could lose some of them. Besides, the least I can do is treat you to a limo. I'll make a call and arrange for you to be picked up out front, here, by five thirty. You'll be home by six. If you want you and your date can use the limo for the evening…my treat," she said, her eyes pleading with me to stay a while longer. "What do you say? We haven't had a heart-to-heart talk in a long time."

Before I could answer, Sophie was on the telephone, ordering a car to pick me up and drive me up to Mount Vernon. It was settled…1, 2, 3…Sophie made up my mind for me and I knew that if I refused her offer, it would be a long argument, and I'd be late getting to the train. Besides, she was right; I had a lot to carry with me.

So Sophie and I sipped coffee and munched on some Danish pastry while Sophie grilled me about my social life at college.

"Have you met anyone special?" she said, zeroing in on her favorite subject…my social life.

I shuffled my feet on the floor, but didn't answer.

"Come on," she said, "out with it!"

I did a lot of hemming and hawing. Finally, I said, "Actually, I was going with a guy I had met in my freshman year. I thought he was the one until this fall. I met a guy on a blind date, Soph. He's very special."

"What do you mean special? What's so special," she said in a dubious voice.

"He's smart, handsome, very gallant," I said.

"Jewish?" she asked.

I nodded. "He doesn't go to Penn State, but he has been showing up every weekend on campus to see me."

"What next?" Sophie said, getting right to the point. "Don't you do anything foolish, Lois. You have to finish college before you think about marriage."

"We haven't even discussed marriage," I assured her. "There's nothing to worry about."

"Not now there isn't," she said. "Is that whom you're going out with tonight? Is this young man in New York?"

"No, I'm going out with someone my parents want me to meet. Roy isn't in New York. He's from Philadelphia. I really don't want to go out with this guy tonight, but my parents insisted, so I'm stuck," I complained.

"Now listen to me," Sophie said, her eyes piercing mine. "Your Mother and Daddy know what's best for you. You go and give this guy a chance. Don't put all your eggs into one basket. This guy…this Roy…he isn't necessarily the right one. You have to meet a lot more guys before you make up your mind. Marriage isn't the end-all you know. Your first priority has to be your education and getting yourself prepared for a career, young lady. Independence! You know how important that is!"

I was not in the frame of mind to hear Sophie go on about how important it was to be self-sufficient. "You can't be foolish, Lois. Wait until the man comes along who thinks a woman is somebody to be looked out for, and not somebody to borrow money from. I looked for him, and I go on looking. For years. If he exists, all I can say is that he and I have never hit the same town together. We're on different circuits. Maybe it will be different for you. I hope so. But you can't concentrate on that. You are at college to prepare yourself for your career. I thought we'd settled that. You obviously have talent as a writer. Your letters are gems, honey," she said.

"But you're prejudiced. You love me, so you think I write well. I don't know if I have the stuff to become a published author," I said.

"Of course you do. I know you do!" she insisted. "And didn't that English professor tell you the same thing last semester?"

I nodded.

"What more proof do you need? But you'll have to get serious about it…start planning ahead. What you'll do once you graduate. You're in no position to even think about marriage, of course," she said with conviction.

The doorman buzzed. Meesa interrupted us. "The car service is waiting to take Miss Lois back," she announced.

"I have to go," I said, relieved to end our little talk. How well I knew what Sophie expected from me, and it was time for me to head back home and make my parents happy by going out with this guy they wanted me to meet.

Sophie grabbed me by the shoulders and planted two kisses, one on each of my cheeks. "Good bye, honey," she said. "And call me tomorrow evening and let me know how you progress with the Christmas cards. I'm going to appear on the Ed Sullivan show tomorrow night, so call me early…around three thirty or four. I'm trusting these to you," she said.

"Don't worry. I said I would get them done, and I will," I assured her.

Of course, I didn't keep Sophie's limo for the evening, but sent the driver back to New York City after he dropped me at home. My blind date with my parent's friends' son, Keith, was a bust. Keith was not my type, and not the gentleman that my parents had assumed he was. In fact, I spent most of the evening pushing him away, especially when he pulled off of the road near the Catacombs, ostensibly to check a possible flat tire. When I realized that he had pulled off of the highway in order to park in a desolate place and make a pass at me, I ordered him to take me home. So much for my parents taste in suitors for me.

All day Sunday I recruited two of my friends from high school who were home for the Christmas break to come over and help with the Christmas cards. My mother also helped. Our dining room table was turned into an assembly line. All the cards that didn't need Sophie's personal notes added to them were stamped and ready to go by four o'clock. The others went into Sophie's carton. I'd take them back to her on Monday.

Their envelopes, too, were addressed and stamped, but not yet sealed. I stood up and stretched.

"I don't want to ever see another Christmas card," I said. "Thanks," I told my friends. "Let's order pizza; I'm starved!"

Sophie was grateful to me for helping her out with her Christmas cards. On Monday afternoon a package arrived for me. In it was a gift from Sophie, a gold cigarette case. Her note said, "Good job! I knew you would not let me down. Happy Holidays! Did you catch me on Ed Sullivan? Call me before you go back to college. Again, thanks and love, Cuz Sophie."

# CHAPTER 15

▼

# WEDDING BELLS FOR ME

*Achieved at great expense and with considerable effort, Sophie Tucker's glamour was potent. Standing on the top rung of the show business ladder, she was dazzling in her beaded dresses, furs, diamonds, and plumed headdresses. Seeing her stunning appearance, audiences often felt they had received their money's worth before Sophie Tucker had sung a note. Her commitment to them was total. During a vaudeville engagement at Chicago's Palace Theatre in 1915, the singer's act ran for thirty-nine minutes. She thrilled her public with sixteen songs!*

*Sophie Tucker mined a rich vein of self-deprecating, sexual, and ethnic humor...all set to music. Though she introduced songs by Walter Donaldson, Richard Whiting, and Irving Berlin, lyricist Jack Yellen and composer Milton Ager provided some of the most typical and successful Sophie Tucker songs during the 1920s.*

I had been taking Sophie's advice and playing the field at college, dating many different fellas until, in the middle of my junior year at Penn State, one of my sorority sister asked me to do her a favor and go on a blind date with a friend of hers from Philadelphia who was a student at Franklin and Marshall College in Lancaster, Pennsylvania.

Since *Sophie and Me* is about Sophie and me this is neither the time nor place to bore you, the reader, with the details of that date or the courtship that followed. Suffice it to say, while Sophie was out of the country doing her grand tour of the world, I fell in love with a blind date named Roy. When Roy showed up for our date, one look was all it took for me to know I wanted to be with him. My young love had seemed so overwhelming, so powerful, then. I would stay awake thinking about him as I lay in my bed.

Roy was a year ahead of me in college and was graduating in June of the end of my junior year of college. He proposed to me over Winter Break, and we planned our wedding a week after his graduation. Roy had been accepted at law school at the University of Chicago the following fall and he wanted me to go with him.

There was no time or opportunity to introduce Roy to Sophie or to get her "expert" opinion, something in retrospect that probably compelled me to rush into marriage behind her back.

When Sophie received our wedding invitation, she called me at Penn State. "Lois," she said, "what's this all about? What about your senior year and graduation?"

I stuttered at first and then said, "I love him, Sophie. You know how it is. This is right for me. I'll finish college somewhere else, don't worry."

"Don't worry? I thought you had better sense," Sophie boomed into the phone.

"Trust me," I said, using the words she often said to me. "You'll love him. If I back out I'll lose him. He's been accepted at the University of Chicago Law School and he wants me to go with him to Chicago."

"Nonsense. If it's meant to be it's meant to be. What's the hurry? Are you pregnant?" she asked.

"I am not," I said, indignation in my voice.

"Well, what is it then? What about your writing career?" Sophie was clearly upset. "His law career is one thing…it's your career you should be concentrating on."

"Just because I'm someone's wife doesn't mean I won't write. After all, you got married three times," I said. As soon as the words were out of my mouth I regretted them.

In May, Sophie responded negatively to my wedding invitation. She would not be able to attend because she would be on tour in Europe.

Our wedding plans proceeded without Sophie, to my disappointment and surprising relief. I pushed away any doubts I myself had about marrying Roy and after a small synagogue wedding in Mount Vernon, during which I found myself at the reception watching the entryway, expecting to see Sophie appear with open arms, only to be disappointed, and a short honeymoon in Puerto Rico, Roy and I moved to Chicago.

Sophie and Moe sent telegraphs on my wedding day (see correspondence section). Sophie's wedding gift to us was her silver Shabbot candlestick holders that I remembered so often graced her Park Avenue dinner table, candlestick holders that I have been using every Friday night since they became mine.

Roy and I promised through sickness and health, until death. At the reception at the synagogue, after the wedding ceremony, Sophie's sister Annie hugged me and kissed both my cheeks. Annie said how lovely I looked and that she hoped we'd be happy. She said Sophie was so sorry that she couldn't make it. I stood there, my lips trembling because I was going to burst into tears, I missed Sophie so much and hoped she wasn't angry. After only a few minutes Annie said she'd better let me go for now, that there were other people to see me. And she said again that I was a lovely bride. Annie clasped my hands, looking directly into my eyes like Sophie always did, and wished me luck.

Then the thought hit me, perhaps Sophie hadn't wanted to see me getting married, that deep down she didn't find it a happy occasion. I feared that she wouldn't want my acquaintance any more.

# CHAPTER 16

▼

# MENTOR

*The fabulous Sophie Tucker has received some great notices for her work in TV and motion pictures, but critics agree that you've never really seen Sophie at all, until you've watched her perform in a nightclub.*

*Her earthy tongue-in-cheek philosophy on men, maids and matrimony is represented by the lighthearted "No One Man Is Ever Going to Worry Me," "No One Woman Can Satisfy Any One Man All The Time" and "Living Alone."*

Once Roy and I were settled in an apartment in Chicago I wrote Sophie a short note to let her know my new address. She wrote me right back and said Annie told her all about my wedding. Annie told her how lovely I looked as a bride. She wrote that she hoped we'd be happy. She said we would meet soon, she was sure we would; we'd have so many things to talk over.

I had such an odd sensation about Sophie, now that I was married. I couldn't find the words to tell her that she'd been my mentor. There was a feeling I had that she thought I was now a wife and lost forever.

In Greek mythology, Mentor was the elderly friend and counselor of Odysseus and tutor of his son Telemachus. In modern English, the tutor's name has become an eponym for a wise, trustworthy counselor or teacher. In that sense, Sophie was my mentor, serving as my guide...a teacher of life and a role model of someone who pursued her personal ambition. Sophie also dared to lampoon the traditional roles of women and men, as well as the sanctity of marriage.

I had a lot of time during Roy's first year of law school. I worked as a secretary in a downtown Chicago office, and, in the evenings, while Roy studied, I listened to Sophie's albums. Her songs seemed to speak directly to me about who Sophie was, what she wanted and how she would not be controlled by any man. Sophie sang out her right to be heard as a woman and that women have appetites, too...sexual ones.

Hearing her voice through my earphones brought Sophie close to me; her words pounded in my ears so that I could imagine that she was with me, in that Chicago apartment, belting out her philosophy to me as a reminder of all she had conveyed to me before my marriage to Roy.

I sat in the apartment all by myself listening to Sophie sing, and I knew, sitting there, that although I was just married, that I was the loneliest girl in the United States. I longed to see Sophie. I didn't want to be shy next time I saw her. I wanted to tell her how much she meant to me, how she had been and still was my mentor.

One day, I knew I couldn't wait until I saw her in person to thank her for her guidance, and I sat down and wrote her a letter. I told her about Chicago, about my senseless job as a secretary. I enclosed a photograph of Roy and me standing in front of the University of Chicago Law School. I confessed that Roy wasn't the most amiable companion but had many good points. I explained my life to Sophie, and how I spent my days. I told her that I think of her all the time and wanted her to know how much I missed our heart-to-heart talks.

I almost signed off when I thought again and added another paragraph telling Sophie that she made me strong, that if it weren't for her telling me time and time again that I could be a writer, I might be satisfied with my boring secretarial job forever, but that it was only temporary while Roy was in law school.

As soon as I walked down to the corner and mailed the letter I felt better. Even if Sophie didn't answer this one, I had gotten off my chest a number of things. Once having written my thoughts, I saw more clearly how, indeed, Sophie was my beloved mentor.

Before Roy's second semester of law school commenced, he decided that law was not for him. We had nothing to keep us in Chicago. His family was in Philadelphia. Roy broke the news to his parents about dropping out of law school, and we made plans to move to Philadelphia where he was going to work in his father's business.

I flew back east that March, and Roy stayed in Chicago to tie up the loose ends, pack up our few belongings, and take care of the actual move to Philadelphia. I went home to my parents' house right before Passover, while Roy stayed behind.

In the back of my mind, I hoped I'd be able to get some time alone with Sophie. The sudden changes in my life of going from single life to wifing, from New York to Chicago, and now from Chicago to Philadelphia ...were overwhelming, and I could use Sophie's level headed thinking to sort things out...if, I prayed, Sophie had forgiven me for ignoring her advice and jumping into marriage before earning my college degree. I didn't want to hear any "I told you so's" from my beloved mentor, for that was how I came to think of Sophie while I lived in Chicago.

# CHAPTER 17

▼

# SEDER AT SOPHIE'S

*The show is "Person To Person," the host Edward R. Morrow. The "Person To Person" camera crew is filming Sophie in her Park Avenue apartment.*

*"And Sophie Tucker, like Queen Victoria, has had her Golden Jubilee," says Morrow.*

*"And here is my Golden Jubilee tablecloth which is made of off color, white linen and all gold applique. Look at this beautiful thing here, Eddie." There on television screens across the world was Sophie Tucker, standing in her Park Avenue dining room. On her dining room table sit silver candlestick holders and a silver bowl overflowing with luscious ripe fruit. Sophie's breathing is a little labored.*

*She holds up the tablecloth. "Isn't it beautiful, Eddie?" she asks.*

*Morrow responds, "It's a lovely thing, Sophie."*

Sophie was appearing on the Ed Sullivan Show an average of three times a year. Whenever possible I caught it on television. But I missed her and hadn't seen her since meeting Roy. Now, I was back East alone, at my parents' house while my husband was still in Chicago. I called Sophie on the telephone. Sophie wasn't home; I left a message for her to call me at my parents'. She called that evening and invited the family for the first night of Passover at her home.

"I'm planning a traditional Seder," she explained. "But not as long as Papa's used to be. Just enough to observe and show respect and, of course, the traditional foods."

Judith and Joel were going to Joel's parents' Seder. So it was Mom, Daddy and I riding the small elevator up to Sophie's apartment on the first night of Pesach. Meesa opened the door when we rang the bell.

Behind Meesa was Moe, puffing on a wet cigar. "Sis!" Moe yelled. "They're here!"

Sophie called from the kitchen, "Show them in, show them in. I'll be right there."

I thought, "How good it is to hear Sophie's raspy voice." I couldn't wait to see her, and ran into her kitchen where I found Sophie with an apron around her waist, hunched over a pot of boiling matza ball soup. She was tasting the soup from a large ladle. I put my arms around her ample waist and rested my head on her back and hugged.

"Sophie, I've missed you. It smells so good in here," I said.

"Here, taste this and tell me if it needs more salt," Sophie said, turning around and sticking the edge of the ladle up to my lips. It was her way of hiding her pleasure at seeing me, and I detected a smile at the corners of her mouth.

I tasted the soup quickly and took the ladle from Sophie's hand. "It tastes perfect!" I said. "And you look perfect. I've missed you, Sophie."

Sophie took me in her arms and gave me one of her super warm hugs that felt like an 'all is forgiven' hug. Sophie took off her apron, squeezed my hand and held it close to her side as we joined the rest of the family in the living room.

Sophie and Moe led the traditional Seder service. Then dinner was served…a sumptuous traditional meal of matza ball soup, kugel, brisket and chicken, lots of matzas and, of course, macaroons for dessert. After stuffing ourselves with too much food, we retired to Sophie's living room. I lit a cigarette.

My mother frowned. "Lois," she said, "you're smoking too much. I worry about you."

Sophie winked at me and said, "When I first smoked in front of my Ma, I watched her face out of the corner of my eye, expecting a scolding. But she didn't say a word. Nor did she mention it during the rest of my visit that time. Sis told me later that after I left she had said to Ma, "What do you think of Sophie smoking?' Ma gave Sis one of her looks and said, 'Who was she fooling? I knew it all the time!' You see, I thought Ma didn't know that I had been smoking behind her back for years, and until that one visit at Pesach I hadn't dared smoke in front of her. After that I smoked frequently in her presence."

My mother was silent.

"No matter how set up I was with myself, the minute I set foot in Ma's house, I had to fall in line with the rules of her old-fashioned, religious household," Sophie continued, and we knew from her tone of voice that tonight she was in the mood to reminisce. "When I was in Ma's house I had to stop being a headliner and the boss, and remember that I was just a daughter. And daughters had to sit back and let the men of the family take the lead. Even Son, the eldest grandson, ranked ahead of me when it came to my parents' house. I nearly choked with pride and tears one Pesach when I was able at the last minute to run home for the Seder. I heard Son ask Pa the four kashas (the traditional four ritual questions which must always be asked by the youngest male at the feast.) The family had moved from Maple Avenue to 160 Barker Street to a two-family house. Mama rented the downstairs apartment to pay the taxes and to give them a little revenue. Upstairs were a living room, dining room, a bedroom for Mama and Papa, and another for Annie. Up in the attic were two more bedrooms, one for you, Moe…remember?"

Moe stood in front of the fireplace and wiped sentimental tears from his eyes. He nodded at Sophie, so she went on.

"Whenever Moe came home, he had that room, and there was another for any relative who came to visit. Annie moved up into this room and gave me her room whenever I visited. Mama was so proud of her house, her little nest, as she called it. She was so proud of her comfortable beds with their big down pillows and feather-filled comforters. And all so snowy white. The whole house was spic-and-span."

Moe broke in, "You could eat off of the floor." Then he nodded for Sophie to continue. Before she did, Charles bid us all farewell and left with Blanche, who was clearly exhausted by the already long night.

By now the rest of us realized that Sophie and Moe were on a memory lane roll; therefore, we sat back, full and satisfied from dinner, and enjoyed their reminiscing.

"Bert sends his apologies. He and Lillian went to her family's Seder back in St. Louis or somewhere," Sophie announced suddenly, as if Bert's absence needed explanation. "Lillian's mother isn't well, and they went to help her prepare for the holidays."

Moe broke in, "Mama wouldn't have anyone in to help her with the housework. Sophie would offer to pay for a maid, but Mama wouldn't have it."

"That's right," Sophie said. "Ours was an Orthodox home, and not one word of criticism could be spoken against the head of the house…Papa. Remember, Moe, there was a spittoon beside Papa's chair at dinner, which he used continuously throughout the meal. This one time, Son, fresh from boarding school, said, 'Grandpa, it isn't proper and it's very bad taste to sit like that and spit during meals.'" Now Sophie herself was laughing and wiping her tears with an oversized pink handkerchief.

"Will I ever forget Papa's face?" Moe roared. "If the ceiling had dropped on him, he couldn't have been more surprised. The four of us and even Mama let out a whoop of laughter. Papa himself was in convulsions, with his mouth full of food."

"Remember, Brother. Even though that spittoon remained handy that meal, Papa obeyed Son and got up and went into the bathroom when he wanted to spit. It was proof of Papa's love for Son that he changed his table manners from that day on."

"We had a kosher home," Moe said, as if to himself. "Of course, ham was taboo in our house."

"Of course," Sophie agreed, nodding vehemently. "Mama had guts— dreisitige. She raised us four kids: Phillip, Annie, Moe and me. Mama's house was always full of women, all Mama's women friends…Mrs. Katzman…"

"And Mrs. Koppleman, Mrs. Susman…" Moe piped up.

"And Mrs. Laschever, Mrs. Gaberman, Mrs. Diwinski and Mrs. Greenberg," Sophie added.

"Ah yes, Ettie Greenberg…I remember her," Moe said, "Ettie was Mama's oldest friend. Mama used to call them 'her committee.' They were always planning how to raise money to build the Jewish Home for the Aged."

"Yeah…" Sophie said. She paused. "You know, it wasn't that I was just after the big money, though that counted, but I had to take care of Son, give him an education and a start in life. But most of all I had to take Mama out of that kitchen. I'd sworn to do both those things, and, by God, I did it."

Moe looked at Sophie with love. "And me…you sent me a money order every week so I could go to Yale."

Sophie threw up one hand to stop him. "I wanted to be sure that your law courses were taken care of. As long as I earned money, you could finish law school. Ma could go ahead and pick out the house she wanted, and Son could go away to a good boarding school, and Annie could have new, pretty clothes and a good time. While I was still in New York Mama would come down and bring Son to spend a day with me. Every time I got to New York in the old days I'd let them know ahead of time and send the railroad fare to Mama or Pa or Anna so they could come down on an excursion ticket and bring Son along. He was growing up so fast…back then he attended kindergarten at the Brown School where I had gone, not a baby any more."

My parents and I sat there, listening to Sophie and Moe go back and forth, all three of us suspecting that this was a catharsis for the two of them, and something they only could indulge in when they had an audience, and an audience where it was safe to do so. I didn't want them to stop. I was learning more about Sophie as I listened.

"Me, too," Moe said. "I went to Brown School."

"Yeah, Brother, we all did," Sophie answered. "Every time I saw my boy I felt I must work harder, get ahead quicker and make more money so I could do more for him. I wanted him to go to a military school where he wouldn't be spoiled. Poor Pa spoiled him at home."

"Sis," Moe objected. "Pa worshiped Son."

"I know, I know, but I was afraid that Son wouldn't get enough discipline if he stayed there. And besides, every time I saw Mama before they moved she seemed older and more bent. She worked so hard to make that damn restaurant pay and to catch up on what Pa lost in those pinochle and poker games. Happy was the day that I was able to get her a home of her own where there was no restaurant business for her any more."

"Ah...Mama...she was some lady," Moe sighed.

My father lit another cigar and sat back in his chair, taking it all in, relaxed and beginning to get sleepy after the big Seder meal.

"You know, when I had my house in Hollywood, I never ran it Hollywood style," Sophie remembered. "I ran it more the way Mama had taught me. There were six of us...hubby (Al Lackey) and I, Ida Cohen, my English friend, who took over the job as housekeeper, Emma, my maid, my niece, Sadie, who drove out with a friend to see California, and the cook. Al and I were still together in those days. We had our ups and downs and our ins and outs, but I wanted to make a go of my married life if I could. Friends were welcomed there at all times for a good home-cooked meal and a game of cards. My Sunday luncheons were mostly for children...Judy

Garland and Freddie Bartholomew would bring their friends and the gang would have a swell time in my pool."

"Judy Garland," I thought. "Wow."

Moe nodded vigorously. "Yeah, Sis, you had Mama's touch."

"Then Pa died," Sophie said, her voice choked with tears.

"Ava shalom…" Moe mumbled.

"I used to run up to Hartford for a few days with the family whenever I could. Ma kept up wonderfully after poor Pa died. From that time on she gave herself heart and soul to the poor. Every afternoon about half past one she would go to the corner and wait for the streetcar to take her downtown for her charity work. By then, the four of us…Phil, Annie, you and I…we gave her a weekly allowance, but at the end of every week she was always broke. She'd give it all away." Sophie wiped her eyes and raked her teeth over her upper lip. "After I hit it big, I sent even more money."

"Sis, remember Ma's coat. I will never forget Ma's joy in her first mink coat." He addressed my father. "Sophie sent it up to her in Hartford and those diamond earrings." Moe took out another cigar, and my father lit it.

Sophie looked at the ceiling, remembering something. "Mama loved it when my friends complimented her on her fine clothes. She'd come to New York and didn't want to miss a thing that my crowd was doing. After my show, when a bunch of us would gather here in my apartment for a poker game that went 'til four or five in the morning, Ma sat up to the very end. The boys would ask her why she didn't go to bed. They'd all call her Mama. She'd answer with her quick, smart mouth, 'No one has to rock me to sleep.'"

"And Mama's hats. Remember how Ma loved hats," Moe said.

"Dressy hats," Sophie agreed. "It was you, Moe, who bought her hats because you could buy the kind she liked, dripping with willow plumes, birds of paradise, flowers, jeweled buckles, and Lord knows what else! After Pa died she spent a lot of time with me when I was in New York, and she'd show off those hats."

"Papa…"Moe said, as if remembering something about their father. "For the first Yartzeit (anniversary) of Pa's death," he added, looking at me now, "Sis and I drove down to London's East End because we were there for his Yartzeit. We drove to a poor little Orthodox shul to say Kaddish ( a prayer for the dead) for Pa. The shul was as old as Methuselah. That's where I met a lot of the Jewish community of London." He turned to Sophie. "Remember, Sis, the Rivoli Theatre in Whitechapel in the East End?"

Sophie nodded. "I do. They had a ninety-five percent Jewish audience at the Rivoli. When I played there they put up a big sign in front that said, 'Welcome, Sophie Tucker, America's Foremost Jewish Actress.' The week I would play at the Rivoli I went to a lot of Jewish restaurants and met all the Jewish actors in London. The food was always good…not as good a Mama's, but good. No one could cook like Ma."

Sophie was weeping openly now. "I still miss Mama,'" she said. "After she died I thought I'd never sing again. Mama always came first to me." Sophie turned to me and pointed her finger. "You can always get success, Lois," she said, "you can always get money, but you can't get another mother. My Yiddisha Mama. Right Marion."

My mother agreed. I smiled at my mother who smiled back at me.

"The whole city of Hartford came out when Mama died," Moe said.

"I was in London and caught a boat back. Remember, Moe, you met me and we took a train to Hartford. I'll never forget that when we got to the street where Mama's house was the road in front of her house was black with crying people. They were Mama's poor. I could hear them wailing as I ran up the stairs to Ma's little nest where the stillness was terrible."

"You were hysterical, Sis," Moe said. "You went running up those stairs yelling that you were home and wanted to see Mama who was already dead. Sis and Phil came to the head of the stairs and said that Ma was still there waiting for you. Mama had made them promise not to put her away until you came home."

Sophie was sobbing now. "My darling Yiddisha Mama knew what it meant to me…how awful I'd feel if I couldn't see her again. She had even set aside her Orthodox belief about a quick burial to spare me. There's nothing she could have done that would have showed me more how much she loved me and how well she understood my love for her."

My father went to Sophie and put an arm around her. "Don't upset yourself, Sophie," he said.

Sophie brushed his arm away. "Nonsense, Milton. It's a cartharsis to talk about Mama and Pa. What are mishpucha for? I wouldn't talk like this in front of strangers."

"You'll disapprove of this, Milton," Moe said, "but Mama had gone to a next-door neighbor and asked the neighbor's daughter to write down her instructions, what she wanted done with her possessions…her will, it was. Mama left her jewelry to Annie. She wanted her fine bedclothing divided between Annie and Phil."

Sophie interrupted Moe. "Mama was careful to explain that if Moe had been married she would have left him some of the bedclothing, but he wasn't. Her mink coat and good clothes she left to her friend Mrs. Ettie Greenberg. Then she had written in her broken English, 'And to my daughter Sophie, who gave me everything, I leave nothing because she don't need anything.'"

Moe and Sophie roared with laughter.

"After Ma died," Sophie said, "I lost my self confidence. I'd had stage fright before, but never anything like I had after Ma died." Sophie paused to wipe away more tears.

Even I had a lump in my throat. I thought about the recording I owned of Sophie singing My Yiddisha Mama. As if reading my mind, Sophie said, "Jack Yellen and Lou Pollack wrote My Yiddisha Mama for me. I introduced it at the Palace Theatre in New York in 1925 and then in the American cities where there was a large Jewish population. At first I was careful to sing it only when I knew the majority of the house would understand the Yiddish words. However, I soon discovered that whenever I sang it here or in Europe, gentiles loved the song and called for it. They didn't need to understand the Yiddish words. People know by instinct what I'm saying, and their hearts respond just as the hearts of Jews and Gentiles of every nationality responded when John McCormack sang *Mother Machree*. You don't have to have an old mother in Ireland to feel *Mother Machree*, and you don't have to be a Jew to be moved by *My Yiddisha Mama*. Mother in any language means the same thing."

"But, Sis, it was always something special when the audience was mostly Jewish, you must admit," Moe said. "Especially when Hitler came to power in Germany. Sis, tell them about Hitler," he said, egging on Sophie.

"Hitler, phooey!" Sophie spat.

"Sis wrote to Hitler," Moe said, addressing my parents and me.

"Okay, okay," Sophie said, agreeing to fill us in. "After Hitler came into power, I heard that he ordered my recordings of *My Yiddisha Mama* smashed and the sale of them banned in the Reich. I was hopping mad. I sat right down and wrote a letter to Herr Hitler. I think my letter was a masterpiece. I told him what I thought of him and his damn anti-Semitism. I gave Hitler a piece of my mind! To this day, I have never received an answer from him."

We all roared with laughter. My father looked at his watch and yawned. "Sophie," he said, "I'm getting tired. I think we'll start home."

Sophie held up one hand. "Just give me five minutes with Lois...alone. I haven't seen her in a long time."

I had noticed that not once did Sophie even ask me about Roy or our marriage. She had been acting as if my life was the same as before; therefore, I wasn't surprised when she requested time alone with me.

I followed Sophie into her bedroom. She patted a place at the foot of her bed for me to sit, and she sat down on a small round stool in front of her dressing table, turning the stool around so that she faced me. She looked me square in the eye. "Tell me, honey, how is married life agreeing with you?"

I wasn't sure how to answer. I hesitated. "It's chaotic right now since Roy and I are moving back east. Roy is still in Chicago handling the physical move. I came on ahead."

Sophie interrupted me. "That's hardly what I meant. Are you happy? You're so young and already a wife. I thought you'd at least finish college."

"I'll finish one day," I said feeling defensive. "I'm relatively happy. Once we're settled in Philadelphia I'll feel better."

No one had ever talked to me so intimately, nor with such urgent regard for my own future happiness. Sophie made me feel that anything, *anything* was possible if I only dared take the chance."

"Listen, you can do anything you set your mind to, be it writing or anything else. It's all in the way you carry yourself," she said.

"I don't know. I don't have the confidence, Sophie," I started to complain.

"It's all a state of mind," she interrupted, "Walk with your head high, and people will think you're more solid, more confident. Carry yourself like the person you strive to be, and people will see you as that person."

"The main thing," Sophie said suddenly, "the main thing is not to settle too quickly. In life...or in love." An immense longing swept into Sophie's face, as if she'd recognized for the first time something about her own life.

I wanted to offer her something, a token of the high regard I had for her. Before I could think of anything, she continued.

"Maybe, Lois, once in a while you have to do something foolish. Just to prove that you're still alive. I don't gloss over or apologize for anything, not even my love life, which I admit set me back a million." She smiled. "I have never discovered why, given the brevity of life and the force of our passions, why people don't pursue their own individual happiness with zeal. I only know that they don't, and that all our goodness, our only claim to glory, resides in this inexplicable devotion to things other than ourselves."

Sophie clasped my hands, looking directly into my eyes, and wished me luck. She didn't say anything about when we would meet again.

At that moment my father came in. "Come on, Lois. Your mother and I are tired. We have a long drive back."

So Sophie and I ended our little heart-to-heart, but I felt sad afterwards, as if I had lost an opportunity to get some good sound advice and also express some of my own doubts as well.

"Take life one day at a time," my mother always said. She didn't understand the pressures that a woman like Sophie faced on a daily basis. There were times when I thought that I might like a simple life like my mother's, even if it meant settling. But that wasn't possible. Not since Sophie's philosophy was tugging at my mind.

# CHAPTER 18

▼

# BACKSTAGE
# AT THE LATIN CASINO

*The fabulous Sophie Tucker has received some great notices for work in televi-*
*sion and motion pictures, but critics agree that you've never really seen Sophie*
*at all, until you've watched her perform in a nightclub.*

*Her stock showmanship, sly wit and warm-heartedness have made her a top*
*drawing card at such famous nightspots as The Latin Quarter in Manhattan;*
*The Beachcomber, Miami; Ciro's, Hollywood; and El Rancho Vegas, Las*
*Vegas, Nevada.*

Roy and I moved to Philadelphia where, thirteen months later, our
daughter Karen was born. Sophie sent Karen a fancy frilly dress and a per-
functory note congratulating us on Karen's birth. Three years later, when
our son Daniel was born, Sophie sent him a gift and me a letter. (See letter in correspondence section)

Those years kept me busy with small children, a household to run, and weekend and evening college courses to study for as I slowly accumulated the credits I would need if I ever succeeded in earning a college diploma. During those same years, Sophie's career was booming, and she was on tour most of the time, traveling throughout the United States and to most places around the world.

One day, when the two children were two and five years old, I received a telephone call from Moe Abuza. Moe informed me that Sophie was going to appear at the Latin Casino in South New Jersey...not far from Philadelphia. Sophie, Moe said, wanted to see me. Could I come to her show and wait around afterwards to visit with her.

I was nervous. Roy and I decided to bring another couple with us, our friends Ellen and Bob Elkins. When we arrived at the Latin Casino, as Moe had instructed, I reported to the box office where four complimentary tickets were left in my name. Sophie was no where in sight, as I had expected, since she was backstage getting ready for her show. A ringside table was reserved for us. The maitre d' escorted us to our places. Each of us ordered a drink. When the waiter brought the drinks to our table I spotted Moe walking towards me. Suddenly my heart was soaring. I jumped up and threw my arms around Moe's neck.

Moe quickly threw his wet cigar into an ashtray and gave me a tight squeeze. "Loey," he said. "Sophie will be so glad that you made it."

"We wouldn't have missed it for anything," I said. "How is Sophie?"

Moe shrugged his shoulders and closed his eyes. "We're getting older, you know. You'll see...she'll knock 'em dead tonight like she always does, but Sophie isn't getting any younger. Often she feels exhausted. But a good show lifts her spirits, and we keep on going."

When I introduced Roy and Bob and Ellen to Moe he barely paid attention. He pinched my cheeks when the lights flickered on and off, and planted a wet kiss on my forehead. "Remember, come backstage after the show. Sophie will be waiting to see you."

Roy and I had stopped to pick up a bouquet of red roses for Sophie. We placed them under my seat during the show. The opening act was a time filler to get the audience warmed up. I hardly paid attention and nursed my drink while I waited for Sophie to come out on stage.

Finally…Ted Shapiro took his place at the piano and the spotlight followed Sophie from the edge of the curtain to center stage where she took a bow, waving her trademark silk handkerchief as she did. The audience hooted, cheered, clapped and rose to its feet. I felt my eyes mist over as I clapped and cheered along with them. I wanted so much to run from my seat and embrace Sophie, but, of course, I sat when everyone else did and enjoyed Sophie's fabulous show.

Several times Sophie winked at me during her performance. I wanted to leap from my seat and run away with her, beg her to take me with her on her world tour. Seeing Sophie in all her glory, luxuriating in a night out at a fancy nightclub, and suddenly feeling young and terribly vulnerable, I wished I could admit my mistakes and turn my life over to Sophie. But, of course, I continued to sit when everyone else did and play the role of happy housewife.

After Sophie sang her final number in the show the crowd went wild and gave her a standing ovation. After three encores and four standing ovations the house lights went on and the show ended.

Roy fished the roses from under our table, and the four of us followed Moe down a back hallway and into Sophie's dressing room.

"Sis, look who's here," Moe said, pushing me ahead of the others in my party.

"Hi, Sophie," I said, suddenly feeling like a stranger.

She nodded at the others with me. "Oh," I said. "Sophie, this is Roy, my husband," I said. Roy stepped forward and handed Sophie the flowers. She handed them to Moe who handed them to an attendant who took them away.

Sophie looked Roy up and down, literally. They awkwardly shook hands.

Ellen and Bob Elkins moved forward. "And these are our friends Ellen and Bob Elkins."

Sophie nodded politely.

"Well, Bob," she said to Roy. "Did you enjoy my show?"

"Yes, ma'am," Roy answered. Before he could correct her about his identity she turned to Bob Elkins.

"And you, Roy," she said to Bob. "I hope you're taking good care of my girl Lois."

"Yes, ma'am," Bob answered, trying not to laugh.

"Well, now. I hope you'll all excuse us for a while. Lois and I haven't seen each other in a long time, and if you three would go back to your table, she and I will be able to talk privately." Sophie dismissed them, and, on cue, Moe led them back out to the cabaret floor.

As soon as we were alone, Sophie said, "I want to talk to you, Loey, but first come closer and give me a kiss."

I gave her a warm, wet kiss on her cheek, loving that Sophie softness and wonderful, sweet clean smell.

"Come sit by me. We haven't had one of our heart-to-hearts in so long," Sophie said. "Your young groom and your friends can have some drinks while they wait."

I pulled a chair up close to her, and she took my hand. "You look good and too young to look old enough to be someone's wife and someone's mother."

I laughed.

Sophie rubbed some cream on her face and with tissues began removing some of the heavy stage make-up. She continued talking to me through the mirror as she scrubbed her face clean. "I'm sorry that I couldn't be at your wedding or the births…or any of it."

"I understood," I said, "you were in Europe on tour. I saw you at Passover before Roy and I moved to Philadelphia and we cleared the air about the wedding. It really was okay, Sophie."

Sophie ignored my reference to having seen me since my wedding and continued as if the talk we had had at her apartment never took place. "And I didn't have enough advance notice to change my schedule," she went on. "So, since I never got to talk to you before your wedding, I want to do it now." She wiped globs of thick make-up off of her hairline and the perspiration from her upper lip. "When you go along for a good many years as I have, you get to sense a right guy from a wrong guy. If experience is any sort of teacher, Lois, then I've had plenty of education. One thing I've learned is how to size up people for what they are. You know the handshake of a regular fella, and you don't fall for the slimy-fish hand-shake. You're on to the quiet guys and the talkative ones who say a lot and yet say nothing at all. I don't know your new husband enough to have an opinion," she hesitated, "Yet...but you know how I don't trust the 'mur-derer'—Judith's husband."

"Joel," I said, filling in the name for her.

"Joel, shmoel, I don't trust him. You know, Al Lackey and I waited and put our wedding off, hoping for a time when he would be established in some business of his own, but it seemed as though that time never would come. We loved each other very much and wanted to be together, so I said to myself, even though it was against my better judgment, why wait? Why let money interfere with two people's happiness? Besides, at the time Al was acting as my personal manager. He was a lot of help to me. He was smart about show business. And so we got married." Sophie's eyes took on an unmistakable intensity, as if she were reliving the moment again.

I wondered what she was getting at and where this conversation would lead us, but I waited patiently.

Sophie kept going. "I married three times. All three ended in divorce. I've said to myself, 'What's the matter with life or with Sophie Tucker, that I've never had a man in my life to stand up to me and give me as good as I could give him? There was Louis Tuck, the boy I married when I was just a kid myself like you. He was the father of my son. Louis was never unkind to me. He never gave me a cross word. But he wouldn't put his shoulder under the responsibility of marriage. I set my mind and my heart on making a career for myself that would make me independent. Independence! That's the key, Lois! Find yourself a career, something… some passion! You're smart; you're beautiful; you're talented. You once wanted to be a writer. Don't settle for being a housewife. You're not the type, I know that."

Sophie's words, for some reason, filled me with fear. I nodded.

"Don't waste time. You had one more year of college to get your degree…did you finish yet?"

"No…but I have been taking credits towards earning my degree," I said, feeling apologetic.

Sophie's eyes narrowed, as if against a blinding light, and I knew that she could sense the upheaval in my mind, no matter how I labored to contain it. I felt certain that she could sense the life I craved.

"Do it, finish college. Then go on. God knows if you are in show business it's a hard thing to achieve a successful marriage. You're always having to pack up and move somewhere else when your married life requires you to be there on the spot. You are always having to go to the theater to put on a show when your husband wants you to sit down and listen to him talk about his business. And, if he has a business and works at it all day, he's too sleepy to pay attention to you when your work is finished around two or three a.m., and you feel like having supper and a game of pinochle…and a little loving. A writer's life is a better life than show biz. More time at home, not away on the road. Read a lot, keep a journal starting now…promise me."

"I promise, Soph," I said.

"I hope you understand why I'm talking to you like this. I believe in you, Lois. I believe that you're destined to be more than just a housewife. Start by finishing your college degree and launching your writing career. An artist…a writer, a singer, a painter…should follow only their passion. All else is a noose around their neck. Become independent and something in your own right." Sophie grabbed both of my hands and held them to her breasts. "Promise me?"

"I promise, Soph," I repeated.

"And if you ever realize that you're not happy being married to Roy, don't be afraid to make a change. You only live once, honey. You get one chance to fulfill your destiny. Don't settle for something less. You promise?"

"I do," I said. "Thank you. For a little time I almost lost myself."

Sophie hugged me, satisfied that she had reached me and made an impact.

As Roy and I drove home that night, I was seized with a restlessness. For the first time, I dimly began to perceive what I really wanted out of life. It was simple. I wanted to answer only to myself, to strike out toward something I didn't know where I was going, only that I had to go in a different direction.

Though it was still night by the time we reached home, it felt like dawn to me.

# CHAPTER 19

▼

# DIAMONDS, DONATIONS & SHOW BIZ ADVICE

*Sophie Tucker's song "Some of These Days" and the way she sang it demonstrate the changes occurring in American music in the first decades of the twentieth-century. This song has become the theme song of Sophie, who uses her powerful chest register to excellent effect. She learned her approach to performing in a long apprenticeship that encompassed a stint at Tony Pastor's $14^{th}$ Street theater with the rag-time pianist Ben Harney and with May Irwin.*

*Tucker's vocal and interpretive mannerisms clearly reflect her continuing association with Black singers and musicians. She plays with the tempo as later singers would do, and there is no subtlety in her singing. She opts instead for dramatic effect, and her robust projection, when heard from the stage of a theater or cabaret, was dauntless and powerful.*

My parents came to Philadelphia for a visit and to see their grandchildren. We had a wonderful Saturday afternoon at the Philadelphia Zoo, and then back to our house for dinner.

After dinner when the children were asleep, my parents and Roy and I relaxed in our living room.

"Daddy," I said. "How's Sophie? Have you seen her lately?"

"She just got back from South Africa," my father said. "Didn't I tell you about that?"

"No," I said, leaning forward. I was eager for news of Sophie.

"Remember Louie Sletowsky, one of my clients who's in the diamond business in South Africa? Well, when Sophie was booked to appear in South Africa, I called Louie and told him that Sophie was coming and that he should help her have a good time. It seems that Louis and his wife fell in love with Sophie. According to Soph, they escorted her around the town, and Sophie secured them front row seats at all her performances. Louie noticed that in one of her shows Sophie wore a headband with a bird of paradise on it. You know, Sophie's into wearing large headdresses at the moment. Anyway, Louie made a pin for Sophie's turban-like headdress with a diamond and a pearl in a lovely setting and presented it to Sophie as a going away present when her South Africa stint ended. Sophie was thrilled!"

My mother added, "Moe was in South Africa with Sophie. It seems that the two of them bought several diamond pieces from Louie. Moe bought Blanche some new additions for her drop-dead collection of baubles."

My father nodded in agreement. "Well, before Sophie left South Africa she made a sizable contribution to one of Louie's favorite charities. I was proud of her. You see, as her tax lawyer I've advised Sophie to give some of her money away for tax purposes."

"I don't believe that's the only reason Sophie is so charitable," my mother objected. "Sophie seems to be continuing where her own mother left off…donating large sums of money to Israel, to Jewish organizations, and back in Hartford to the charities that meant so much in her mother's life."

"Oh, wait a minute," my father said, reaching for his wallet from his trouser pocket and removing a newspaper clipping. "This," he said, handing the article to me, "appeared in the *Hartford Times*:

*Sophie Tucker, Composer*
*To Be Honored Here April 3*

*Emanuel Synagogue will honor two of its members who attained top rank in the entertainment world. They are Sophie Tucker, the last of the "red hot mamas," and Harold Rome, author of many hit songs in several outstanding musical comedies. Both are Hartford natives.*

*Miss Tucker and Mr. Rome will highlight a "gala evening" planned by the synagogue in its new religious school and auditorium on Mohegan Drive, West Hartford, Sunday evening, April 6.*

*Police Court Judge Alfred F. Kotchen, general chairman, announced that both entertainers have informed Rabbi Morris Silverman they would be delighted to star in a benefit performance for the school's building fund.*

*Except for occasional visits to friends and relatives, Miss Tucker has made few public appearances in this city since she went on to fame and fortune.*

"May I keep this?" I asked my father.

"Sure, go ahead. Sophie would want you to have it," he answered.

At the time I didn't realize that that appearance in West Hartford marked the beginning of Sophie's last six years and her dedication to giving back to society all that she could, especially in her home town and to the causes that her mother had worked so selflessly for. Sophie never forgot Hartford. It was her home.

That year, Sophie, in a speech at a New York benefit dinner, said, "Charity has become my life. For the past forty years I have been receiving; now I'm going to do some giving."

At the time I didn't know that this would turn out to be something of an understatement. Before she died, Sophie would have given more than $600,000 to all types of charity. In Hartford she would appear at synagogues and public auditoriums to, as she said, "do some giving." She gave thousands of dollars to Jewish organizations alone. Even after her death her charitable work would continue.

Sophie's pet project was the Hebrew Home for the Aged in Hartford, to which she would later leave an additional $10,000 in her will. This was the very home that her mother had helped to found at the turn of the century.

In addition, Sophie would leave $30,000 to the Sophie Tucker Foundation and $25,000 to her friend and pianist Ted Shapiro, and ten bequests totaling $89,000. Before her death Sophie set up two youth centers in Israel bearing her name.

Sophie planned to give most of her wealth away before and after her death, and to leave the remainder of her estate to Son, Brother and Charles.

The esteem in which Sophie is held had been exemplified by the record-breaking testimonial dinner that had been given in her honor by the Jewish Theatrical Guild to inaugurate her Golden Jubilee Year...the same year that she dipped her silverware into gold. Legend has it that the banquet hall of the Waldorf Astoria in New York never held such a throng of notables. The event was not only a tribute to Sophie Tucker the stage star, but also to Sophie Tucker the woman, who devoted the evening of her life to aiding those in need, regardless of race or religion. From the sale of her book and her Mercury recordings, Sophie contributed hundreds of thousands of dollars to worthy charitable causes. In addition, many of the dinners given in celebration of her Golden Jubilee netted immense sums of money that Sophie donated to such causes. At another dinner given in her honor in Hartford, a million and a half dollars was raised for the Hebrew Home for the Aged.

"Giving is a part of show business," Sophie said. "Besides, darling, everybody knows you can't take it with you!"

Money wasn't the only thing that Sophie gave away. To each generation with stars in their eyes, she gave out top-notch advice on how to be a success in the profession, as she called show biz.

To singers who asked her advice Sophie said, "Get new songs. Pay a writer to write them for you. Get songs that you can make your own.

Don't copy other singers. Don't sing their songs. Don't do their stunts. Don't make your act a carbon copy of someone else's. Not if you want to succeed. If you want to stay in show business more than a season or two, put off buying that mink coat or diamond bracelet and buy songs instead. They'll pay you dividends and cost nothing for insurance and storage.

"In show business everything is important. Your way of walking on the stage, your manner, how you hold your hands, turn your head, bow…all these are a part of your act, and as important in their way as the song you sing or the lines you read.

"Show business is a business, and a hard-boiled one. If you're in it, it is up to you to protect yourself. No one else is going to do it for you. And there's no room in show business for hurt feelings, resentments, or self-pity. Success in show business depends on your ability to make and keep friends. Entertainers who last are the ones who aren't standoffish and high-hat. To hold your audience, you've got to give something of yourself across the footlights. That something has got to be genuine, sincere. You might be able to fake it for a season or two…maybe. Then the public gets wise and gives you the razzberry. And you're done. Washed up! And you've got to dress smart. It helps."

A month after my parents' visit, I came to New York to see Judith and Joel and their three children. It was their daughter Jennifer's birthday. I arranged for Roy's parents to stay with Karen and Daniel, and took a train to New York City. I spent the first two nights in Mount Vernon. I called Sophie on the third day and we made a date to go poking around New York City with a car and driver.

The last time I had seen Sophie was backstage at the Latin Casino in New Jersey. Having a day with her in New York was a rare treat for she seemed to be travelling more and more frequently, and since I had a family of my own I was less available.

Sophie was dressed in a navy suit when she let me into her apartment. "So what's on our agenda today?" she asked, giving me a warm hug.

"I'm game for anything," I said.

"I thought we'd do a little shopping this morning. Are you up for something like that?" she asked.

"That's what I was hoping you'd say," I responded.

"Good, that's good," Sophie said. "Let's go. We have some shopping to do. We've got to get you looking like a new woman."

Shopping with Sophie was an experience. Once we got to 57th Street, we spent the rest of the morning in a variety of shops. I bought a new outfit before Sophie dragged me into a lingerie shop. Sophie went absolutely wild in there. Not for herself, of course, but for me. She would pick up lacy, see-through underwear and matching bras off the racks and hold them up for me to evaluate.

"This looks pretty steamy," she'd say.

I couldn't help but laugh whenever she did it. Sophie's lack of inhibition was one of the things I loved most about her. She really didn't care what other people thought, and I often wished I could be more like her. After taking two of Sophie's suggestions the two of us spent a couple of minutes in a bookstore.

When we returned to Sophie's apartment, we collapsed on the sofa and drank iced coffee.

Sophie rested her elbows on her knees. "So…have you been doing any writing?" she asked.

"Journal writing mostly. But," and I paused for dramatic affect. "But, Soph, in June I will have my college degree."

Sophie clapped her hands with delight. "That-a-girl! But you still haven't answered my question. Your writing?"

"As soon as I receive that diploma I plan to buckle down to some serious writing. I promise, Soph."

"Listen, honey, in 1945 I wrote my autobiography. It was a long, slow business to write down everything I could remember, writing it by hand, usually late at night after I came home from work. I had no time off for writing. As a matter of fact, once I started that book I worked harder and steadier than I'd worked in years. If I could do it you can. I never went to college, so you're a step ahead of me."

"I doubt that," I said, and I meant it.

"I like your pants suit. Stand up," Sophie ordered.

I did, doing a ballet turn to show off my new outfit.

"Did you know that it was me, not Marlene Dietrich, who introduced women wearing pants in this country?" Sophie said.

I shook my head.

"Well it was, and I'm damn proud of it. Now it's chic for you to walk around in a pants suit like the one you're wearing. It's not easy to be a success in any profession, you know. You must expect to make sacrifices and to work to get ahead. Doesn't a nurse have to study and work hard? Think of the years of work that go into the making of a physician. It's the same for writers."

"Well, tell me some of the secrets that helped you do it," I said, encouraging Sophie to talk.

"I've been asked many times how to get ahead in show business. I can only speak about show business...I don't know about writing. First, always be on time. If you're in show business, you can never afford to be five minutes late. Especially when you're starting out you've got to be on time or you'll get fired. After that it gets to be habit.

"Second, be sure you look good. The performer never has any time off. There never is a day or an hour when you can afford to slump. You never know whom you may meet, and you've got to be ready. You can't afford to be passed over because you didn't make up properly that day or you were careless about your clothes, or didn't keep the appointment with the hairdresser the day before.

"Third, be individual. Don't make yourself a carbon copy of some other entertainer or some glamour girl of the screen. One of the saddest things in show business is the number of girls working in cafes in every town of any size who look, dress, and sing alike. You can't tell one from the other. Not one of them will ever get anywhere in show business until she breaks away from that pattern, until she sings something original.

"Fourth, making a success calls for plenty of patience and tolerance. You can't afford to hold resentments or grudges. They'll interfere with your work. And first, last, and all the time, it's your work that counts. The same holds true for writing. So, what about it?"

Sophie was tireless in badgering me. "What do I know about professional writing?" I whined.

"Listen, sweetheart, all my piano playing was always done with one finger. When I started out I couldn't read a note of music. I can't to this day. But I always knew how to work hard. And I can pick out the winners because they're always the hard workers. I worked with Judy Garland in the movie *Broadway Melody*. Judy was the only one in the whole cast in whom I saw great possibilities. I told L.B. and everyone on the lot that Judy, if carefully handled and groomed, would become a big MGM star. The rest, of course, is history. My prediction was right. It took hard work. Every night after work, at three or four in the morning, I would put in an hour or two studying new songs before I went to sleep. Every afternoon from four to five Ted and I rehearse. It's a full day. Living like that you don't have much time for energy, for a personal life."

I looked at my watch.

"Don't tell me you have to go so soon?" Sophie complained.

"I have to get back for the kids," I said

Sophie took out a cigarette and lit it. "One more cigarette. Let's have one more cigarette," she said. She rolled the end of her cigarette around on her fingers and added, "My doctor is trying to get me to give these cancer sticks up, you know. I don't think I can do it. It's my one remaining vice." She gave a deep Sophie laugh that set off a bout of coughing. She took a sip of her iced tea and was quiet.

"Are you feeling okay, Soph?" I asked. I noticed that she looked tired, older, still stunning and well groomed, but definitely worn out.

"I feel fine. I just choked on some smoke, that's all," she said, waving a dismissive hand in my direction.

"You're young, Loey. I'm an elder statesman in show business. The young people in show business today lack something we all had...it's the combination of humility and push. . . . the feeling of humbleness and the push to do the things that have to be done, to learn by hard, hard grinding work the things that get you up on top and keep you there. But if you go out and ask a hundred of these kids in show business what I'm talking about, only one of 'em will know...and I can tell you her name. About ten years ago, down in Miami Beach, I met this little girl, sort of a Scarlett O'Hara type. She asked me to drop over and take a look at a movie she was in, and since her father-in-law owned the café where I was working at the time, I put myself out. On the hottest day of the year, I went over to the picture house in Miami...and I'll never forget what I found.

"Out in front of this theater was the girl's name in lights—five feet high! The publicity department of some movie company was shoving her down the public's throat...some press agent had decided to make this little girl a star!"

The way Sophie ripped out the words "press agent" rattled the hundreds of pictures of her own spectacular career on the walls around her, and the glass shook in the frames as her anger mounted. "Darling, that is not my kind of show business! I worked hard, terribly hard for years and years before I saw my name up in lights. I fought my way up from the 10-cent theaters to the 25-cent theaters, to the 50-cent theaters, and finally up to the top—the Palace. I started in blackface because some managers thought I was ugly, and I wore blackface until some guy called me a good-looking dame and then I showed my face. But my name never got put up in lights by any press agent...the public put Tucker up there!

"This was something that little girl didn't know anything about. And when I saw her on stage inside the theater, it was even worse than seeing her name in lights...a girl in ugly gowns with her beauty hidden under layers of awful makeup. She didn't go over at all.

"It pained me to give her my opinion, but she asked for it and she got it: 'How do you people dare to appear before the public with so little? Where do you get that much nerve?' Oh, I gave that kid the most awful lashing, and her chin hit the floor as she listened. Darling, I can hurt people, and hurt 'em bad. Sometimes without really wanting to, I'm very ruthless and cruel and mean. I was double mean this time, because of what they had done with, and to, this girl. Here she was given a golden opportunity...the kind nobody ever offered me at her age...and she was so pitifully unprepared for it...she had nothing to give in return.

"After that lashing I gave her I never expected to see her again...but she fooled me. Shortly before my New York opening, I was at Madame Francis' having my $1,500 gown fitted for the show, when that same little girl came running up to me. This time, she was wearing an elegant dress and she looked lovely...so different. I didn't know who she was at first. And she told me: 'Aunt Sophie, it took a little while, but now I understand what you told me back in Miami. I've started over again, and I'm going to work and work and work until I make it the right way!' And darling, it looks like she meant it...she's left her husband back in Florida, while she's working on the road, and maybe you've seen her on the screen . . . Janice Paige. She's one youngster I know who has the guts, and I hope the talent, to reach the top."

After our last cigarette, I gave Sophie a firm hug and said, "I love you, Soph."

"I love you, too, Loey. We both know that. Now get on home to your family and remember everything we've talked about today. Independence! Your independence, dear, will come from your becoming a great writer. I know that for sure!"

Among the pictures of Sophie on the walls of her Park Avenue apartment, where all the treasures she had collected and stored in warehouses for forty years had now found a home, she pointed out in passing as she walked me to the door her own three husbands. "Taking your husband along with you on the road is no good...you got no time for worries when you're working! I learned that the hard way. Janice Paige learned that. I know show business, better than I know the literary life…but it may also be a lesson for you, Loey, once you launch your own career as a writer."

Sophie planted a wet kiss on each of my cheeks. "I figured you'd come see me again when you were ready," she said.

"I thought I was keeping things under control," I said.

"Perhaps for other people. But I've known you long enough to know when something's up with you." Sophie smiled. "Enough of neglecting yourself. If everyone who thought they might fail didn't even try, where would we be today? I'm older than you, and I've gone through a lot. One of the things I've learned in my life is that sometimes you've got to take a chance."

"You make this sound so easy," I said.

"Your vision, as they say, has become clouded. It is easy," Sophie said, and she pushed me forward. "Now remember what I said, and go back and get to work," she said, affectionately.

And I rode the metroliner train home to Philadelphia with those words ringing in my ears.

# CHAPTER 20

▼

# BLACKFACE

*But the ambitious girl had her sights set on a higher target. Amateur night in a Harlem theater offered an opportunity to sing from a stage instead of from a cafe floor. The man who conducted the contest appraised her as she waited in the wings.*

*You're too ugly to go on as you are," was his edict, and hurriedly Sophie's face was smeared with burnt cork and a bandana wound around her head. The make-up was not inappropriate back then. White performers were then emulating the singing of "colored folks," and Sophie's voice was aptly suited to what was then called "coon-shouting."*

*She coon-shouted her way that night to her first vaudeville engagement. An agent in the audience offered to book her, and Sophie promptly gave up her job in the German Village, where her tips often amounted to a hundred dollars weekly, and began journeying from one small town to another at a salary of twenty-five dollars a week. For the next two years, life was a succession of railroad jumps, shabby furnished rooms, greasy restaurants and dilapidated op'ry houses.*

*So after her fifteen-a-week job singing up to a hundred songs a night at the rathskeller and as a black face singer, Sophie Tucker's wanderings led to New York and a fateful engagement at Tony Pator's, where Gus Hill, a burlesque impresario, came backstage and offered her an engagement with "The Gay Masqueraders."*

*We Shall Overcome* is a Baptist hymn which became the anthem of a social movement. The sixties gave impetus to reform, and tried to combine the quest for social justice with the search for personal authenticity. The watchword of the sixties was *liberation*: the shackles of tradition and circumstance were to be thrown off.

The arts often represent the opinion in the culture as a whole...thus there have been changes in the arts—shifts in consciousness, and changes in society.

In 1963 Martin Luther King told an historic rally in Washington that he had a dream. Two years later, thanks to pressures of the civil rights movement, racial injustice was eating away at my consciousness. For me, a succession of marches and demonstrations were like learning a new language. One of the ironies of the sixties was that protest was now a middle-class phenomenon. For me there was one rude personal shock. I confronted Sophie on the telephone.

"How could you?" I asked, referring to Sophie's first show business triumph as a blackface performer.

"I only wore that disguise by accident," Sophie answered. "Now don't rush to judgment. This is going to be a long phone conversation, so you'd better settle back and listen, and listen good." I heard the apprehension in Sophie's voice. It was probably the first time I had expressed such disappointment in her.

"Okay, I'm listening," I said.

"When Chris Brown, the manager of the amateur night at a Harlem theatre, spotted me preparing to go on, he shouted to an assistant, 'This one is so big and ugly. Better get some cork and black her up.' I protested to no avail. It was another time…another era. Within weeks I was booked on the small-time vaudeville circuit, for the next six years, from 1906 to 1912, I was the World Renowned Coon Shouter."

"The what? I can't believe it!" I said.

"It was the first part of the twentieth century, Loey. You must have perspective. I was one of the first female entertainers to use blackface. It worked as well as it did for Eddie Cantor and Al Jolson, who were Jewish, and for Bert Williams, a West Indian. After a while I began to use high yellow rather than jet-black. When I'd pull off one of my gloves and show that I was white, there'd be a surprised gasp, then a howl of laughter. So I began interpolating Yiddish words, at first to give the audience a kick but also to declare who I really was." She paused. "Are you still listening?"

"I am. How could you take such crap? You were never too ugly… you…."

"Wait a minute…wait a minute…I was unsure of myself, young, and determined to get work and to win that amateur night. If I resented the blackface, it was because it prevented me from appearing as myself, like the prettier girls. Blackface denied my femaleness," Sophie explained.

I was aware that she was saying little about the racial stereotyping endemic in such a costume, in the minstrel gestures and lyrics that were part of her act. But I listened.

"The style was ubiquitous in vaudeville, inherited from the popular minstrel shows of the nineteenth century. For we Jews like me and Jolson and Cantor we were eager to show that we were real Americans. We were considered ethnic entertainers…Jews. *Coon* singing had benefits. With African-Americans…that's the right term isn't it?…the butt of our humor, immigrant vaudevillians like us demonstrated that however foreign our own cultures might be viewed, blacks were even more inferior. Well, not inferior, but different. Blackface also embodied a plaintive note expressing the pain of rootlessness so deeply a part of our immigrant experience. Do you understand what I'm saying to you?"

"The more you explain, the worse it sounds, Sophie. Coon? That's a horrible term," I protested.

"Listen to me. Although blackface molded my performance style, enhancing the physicality of my performance and introducing me to the modern syncopated style of music that would facilitate my later embrace of jazz; I chafed at its restrictions and denial of my femininity. Yet I was afraid, in those days, to go on stage without it. The opportunity to discard blackface arose later on when a Brooklyn theater manager, pretending that my trunk was lost, sent me on stage without it. From that day forward I never performed in blackface again. I was relieved to be done with it!"

"I would think so," I said sarcastically.

"Listen, I wasn't and have never been a racist. My best friend was a Black woman…Mollie. Did you know that?" Sophie was shouting now in her own defense.

"Mollie? This is the first time you've mentioned her. If she's your best friend, how come I've never met her?" I challenged her. Then added, "It's like saying 'some of my best friends are Black or Jewish or whatever."

"You never met her because she's dead, that's why." Sophie said, ignoring my last comment. "When I was in the Follies my dressing room was next to Lillian Lorraine and her colored maid…a handsome woman. One night I was very lonesome, the other girls in the Follies ignored me. I went into the next door dressing room where Lillian's maid was and poured out all my worries and fears to her. Her name was Mollie Elkins. She reassured me that in every show one kid was always ignored…was the *patsy*. That night I told Mollie about Son, who I told her was the cutest little fellow and that I had to make it for him. From then on, Mollie called me Patsy. She told me to keep my chin up and that she'd root for me. Mollie's friendliness cheered me up. Her confidence in me gave me the courage to do well that first night of the Follies of 1909. After the show that night Mollie threw her arms around me and said, 'You were great, Patsy. From now on you're going places!' And I told her that when I did, she was going with me. I told her that she and I would go all over the world together.

And we did until her death. We went through a lot together..." Sophie was crying now. "Are you still there?" she asked.

"I am. What happened next?" I asked, lost in her story.

"The star of the Follies, Nora Bayes, however, was jealous of the audience response to me and she threatened to leave the show if I stayed and stole the limelight. I told Mollie about it, and she told me to go home and get some sleep and report for rehearsal at ten the next morning. Outside the theater that evening I found Irving Berlin waiting for me. I poured out the story of Nora Bayes to him and Irving said, 'Listen, kid, this is show business. You know what you did tonight, don't you? After this, there's no stopping you. You're going places, young lady. Only yours will be the hard way. And remember, the hard way is the best way. I have to go back to New York tonight. Keep in touch with me. Let me know what happens.' And Irving was one. So at rehearsal the next day Mr. Ziegfeld took away all my numbers except one to placate Nora Bayes. Mollie calmed me down and told me that there would be other shows. 'Do your one song great, Patsy,' she said, 'and you'll see. If you've got the goods, and you have, there's nobody can take your chance away from you.' Mollie kept me from feeling bitter.

"When I left the Follies, Mollie and I stayed friends. She took me under her wing and never let me forget that she was my friend whose faith in my ability to get somewhere never wavered. It was Mollie who insisted on my going to a doctor when my throat tightened up. She paid for the visits and for the medicine. Over and over Mollie said that I couldn't afford to let myself get bitter. Mollie and her husband Bill looked out for me 'til I got better. They bought me and Moe food. It turned out Mollie's extra money came from the money she won at the horses. She played the horses...two-dollar bets...and was lucky. Out of her winnings she kept Moe and me. Mollie gave me the courage to pull myself together, overcome fear and lack of confidence and impress William Morris. She forgave me for having once gone on in blackface. Why can't you?"

"Well, I understand, but I'm still..." I began.

"Still what? I'm not done yet. When I auditioned for William Morris singing *My Southern Rose*, I realized I hadn't arranged with the prop man to have a chair ready on stage for me to lean on. Once on stage I yelled for Mollie to bring me a chair for the number. Out came Mollie, toddling to her own humming and smiling as she brought out a chair. The audience ended up loving her. At the end of my act I yelled, 'Come on, Mollie, and take a bow. You're part of my act now.' And she was. And until Mollie's death, which almost did me in, she and I were inseparable, like sisters. I still miss her. As a matter of fact, young lady, my theme song *Some of These Days* is one thing more I owe to Mollie.

"I was riding high in Chicago and one day Mollie came to me with her mad up. 'See here, young lady,' she said, 'since when are you so important you can't hear a song by a colored writer? Here's this boy Shelton Brooks hanging around for you to hear his song and you give him the run around.' I hadn't been aware of Brooks before and agreed to hear his song. The minute I heard *Some of These Days* I knew it was for me. Later Brooks wrote *Downtown Strutters Ball*, which I also sang. After that, Black song-writers spread the word that I gave Black songwriters a chance. I made it up over the years…fighting for Black entertainers' rights…donating large sums of money to Black causes.

"For your information, it was well known in the Black show business community that Sophie Tucker gave Black composers a chance. I gladly featured and still feature songs by Black writers. When I sang these songs they became hits and then standards.

Now do you understand that I'm not a racist?"

I was silent.

"Are you there or did you hang up?" she shouted into the telephone.

"No—I'm still here," I said.

"Perspective, Lois, my dear, you must look at events in their historic context. Blackface entertainers were not necessarily racists then. Today it would be something else, we now know better, of course. Give me the benefit of the doubt, will you?"

And, of course, I did. This was Sophie, my mentor, my role model. I couldn't let this come between us.

In the fall of 1998, while writing this chapter for *Sophie and Me*, the following article appeared in *Lilith* Magazine. It tied the tradition of African-American women blues singers to Sophie Tucker's style, both traditions emanating from women outsiders in American culture.


## APPETITES: BIG MOUTH, BIG SEX

*When I think Big Mouth, I think Sophie Tucker, one of the early "mothers" of a long line of Jewish women. Big Mouths on stage. In helping to create an American cabaret night life, she made loudness, power and sex synonymous by the 1920s. Her enormous voice, in the same tradition as great African-American women blues singers, crooned about wanting sex from her man...a deeply scandalous message that, more than once, got her arrested. Tucker also dared to lampoon the traditional roles of women and men, as well as the sanctity of marriage.*

*Tucker was part of a generation of "outsiders" who, for the first time, were flocking to cities, either as a result of the Great Migration or of immigration to America. Jews and African-Americans were creating something entirely new: a hot, jazzy urban culture. They toppled Victorian turn-of-the-century norms about propriety and the denial of pleasure. Female entertainers like Tucker asserted, through their bold presence on stage, that women have appetites, that they can risk taking public roles. They can sing about who they are, what they want, and how they will not be controlled by any man. But Tucker's loud mouth also, remarkably, sang about something very different. "My Yiddishe Mama"...her signature song...became, for generations of Americans, the embodiment of longing for the lost Old Country, symbolized by devoted Jewish motherhood. As Jewish "outsider," Tucker expressed both scorn for what seemed to her to be the "emptiness" of propriety, as well as complicated bereavement towards a world to which the "outsiders" would never return.*

*Tucker's big mouth shouted out her right, as an American Jewish female, to be heard...no matter what, she said. A long line of great entertainers...Fanny Brice, Totie Fields, Joan Rivers, Bette Midler and many others...are her descendants. They are all-star "transgressors" who contributed to redefining American culture.*

*——Riv-Ellen Prell,*
*anthropology professor, University of Minnesota*

# CHAPTER 21

▼

# SOPHIE IS SICK

*The Latin Quarter, New York City, October 17, 1965. The buzzing hushed, the blue mist hovered over shadowy tables as the gleaming cone of light focused on the Grand Old Lady of Song. Bespangled and dazzling, she segued easily into her finale, her bright blondness like swirls of yellow taffy atop her ample outline, the glittering dots of her gown shimmering as she swayed slightly to the beat.*

On a Monday afternoon in November of 1965, my father strolled from his Manhattan law office to Sophie's apartment for lunch. There was nothing that he liked better. He and Sophie had developed a special relationship. Sophie was twenty plus years his senior and sometimes like an older sister, or aunt or mother to him. He often played the role of counselor to her...both as a lawyer and as a personal confidante.

Sophie was still in her bathrobe when he arrived at her apartment. The maid, Meesa let him in and led him to the study, where Sophie was sitting at her desk, a cigarette burning in the ashtray and the telephone receiver to her ear.

My father kissed the top of Sophie's head in greeting and sat down while she wound down her telephone conversation. When she hung up, she started to cough, a hacking cigarette cough.

My father reached over and put out her cigarette in the ashtray. "You smoke too much, Soph," he said. "I don't like the sound of that cough."

"It's too late for me to stop smoking, Milt. I'm hooked and too busy to start going through nicotine withdrawal."

He noticed dark circles under Sophie's eyes. She looked tired, worn out. "Are you getting enough sleep? You look beat," he said.

"I think I'm getting too much sleep. Look at me…it's lunchtime and I'm still not dressed. I slept late this morning, which isn't like me at all. I've been exhausted lately. But don't start with me on giving up smoking. It's my one remaining vice these days and I enjoy it too much to give this one up."

"I'll lay off for now," he conceded. "Will your schedule lighten up around Thanksgiving? Maybe you can take some time off."

"It's one of the busiest times for me. Vegas, New York, Miami…a lot of my loyal fans vacation over Thanksgiving and Christmas. I have a rough winter schedule coming up," she said, suppressing another bout of coughing with her fist.

Meesa appeared in the doorway. "Lunch is ready, Miss Sophie," she said.

"Already? I'm not even hungry," Sophie answered.

"I am, and I have to get back to the office in about an hour," my father said.

"Then let's go in and eat lunch," Sophie said, standing and taking his arm as he escorted her into the dining room.

Meesa set a bowl of chicken soup in front of my father, thick with chicken, carrots, celery and giblets…the way he liked it. She set a cup of clear chicken broth in front of Sophie.

"What's a matter, Soph, are you dieting?" he asked.

"My stomach has been upset lately, so I've been sticking to clear broth and saltine crackers. Don't worry about me, I have enough fat to live off of for awhile, anyway," Sophie said. She laughed until her laugh turned into another coughing spell.

"I want you to call your doctor, now, while I'm here," my father said firmly. "Maybe you picked up a bug somewhere, but you sound awful and you look exhausted."

"Nonsense! I'm as strong as an ox. I just have a little stomach virus and the cough is probably some kind of an allergy," Sophie said, waving her hand at him.

"If that's the case, then your doctor will prescribe some medicine and you'll be fine in a few days. You can't do your act in this condition…what if you have a coughing fit?"

"You're really worried, Milt, aren't you?"

"I am. And I insist you listen to me!"

"Okay, okay…just to make you happy, I'll call Dr. Cohen," she said.

"No, before I leave," he insisted.

Meesa brought a telephone into the dining room and plugged it into the wall so that Sophie could telephone Dr. Cohen from the table. They set up an appointment for four o'clock that very afternoon.

"I'll call you before I leave the office to go home," my father said when he was leaving. "Or you call me after you see Dr. Cohen. I won't be leaving my office until after six. You promise?"

"Yes, yes. I promise. You're an old worry wart, you know that," she said.

At six fifteen Moe telephoned Daddy at his office and told him that Dr. Cohen had admitted Sophie to Mount Sinai Hospital because she had a nasty intestinal inflammation. Dr. Cohen said that he didn't want to fool around with it, and hospitalizing Sophie was the only way he could be sure that she followed his orders. While she was at Mount Sinai, according to Moe, Dr. Cohen would order a battery of tests done on Sophie since she hadn't had a complete physical in years.

"Sophie will probably stay in the hospital until Friday," Moe said. "That will give them time to do the tests and clear up her intestinal inflammation."

"Is Sophie willing to do this?" Daddy asked.

"Believe it or not, she's acting like the perfect patient. I have some engagements to cancel for her, but other than that Sis is pretty passive about it and almost seems relieved to be confined to total bed rest," Moe explained.

Sophie's five-day hospital stay turned into several weeks. When she came home from the hospital, the newspapers reported that she was recovering well from an intestinal inflammation. But, we soon learned, Sophie's intestinal inflammation turned into lung cancer and kidney disease.

My parents kept me updated on Sophie's condition. I called Sophie every week, and begged her to let me come to see her.

"I forbid it!" she boomed at me over the telephone.

"Why? Maybe you'll feel better if you have me around to badger," I teased.

"Very funny. You, young lady, stay home and take care of your family and your own career. I'll take care of mine," Sophie barked.

"Don't get so damn pushy," I said, chuckling. But I knew that Sophie didn't want me to see her. As I set my dinner table each evening I'd think of Sophie and the wonderful meals at her apartment. I began keeping the silver candlestick holders out on the dining room table with two long tapered candles in each. In the middle, like Sophie's, I kept a silver bowl overflowing with fresh fruit and nuts. It made me think of Sophie for whom I prayed nightly would recover from her illness.

Sophie went back to the hospital for chemotherapy but demanded to be brought back to her apartment afterwards. Then, a month later she underwent radiation treatment. Again, she insisted on being an outpatient and sleeping at home during her last four months. Sophie was now confined to a wheelchair with round-the-clock nurses. Only close family members were allowed to visit...Moe, Charles, Son, and my father were her most frequent visitors.

Sophie was a fighter and fight she did, trying chemotherapy, radiation, and any known cure that might save her life. To see her in her final days was heart breaking. Wracked with lung cancer and undergoing chemotherapy she was thin, exhausted. When she lost all of her hair she wore a wig.

But Sophie never gave up her fight…the fight to live just as her early life focused on her fight to make a name for herself in show business. She more than won her first fight, but even Sophie Tucker couldn't win the final, inevitable fight with death.

# CHAPTER 22

▼

# SOPHIE TUCKER DIES

## FEBRUARY 9, 1966

*"You're gonna miss your mama, your big, fat mama, your Red Hot Mama, Some of These Days."* *The crescendoing applause roared and swelled to a drown out. A smile, a salute to her audience, and her song had ended. But nobody knew it then.*

Sophie Tucker died Wednesday, February 9, 1966 in her Park Avenue apartment at age 82. When my parents called to tell me my first thought was that it had to be a mistake. I felt sick to my stomach. Time ceased to exist. I struggled to accept that Sophie wouldn't ever again break into the smile that I loved. I stood there, after that telephone call ended, and made a low, keening sound. No mistake. Sophie was gone. I started to cry. My sobs deepened. I wandered from room to room in my Philadelphia home, on legs that were wooden, muscles that were tight. The memory of her scent led me, the echo of her voice followed.

I took out the silver candle stick holders that she had given to me and placed them on the kitchen counter. I placed two long white candles in them and lit them both as I recited Kaddish, the Jewish prayer for the dead.

The first funeral took place in New York City's Riverside Funeral Chapel, 76th Street and Amsterdam Avenue, but Sophie wanted to be buried in Hartford, her home. Thus, friends and show business acquaintances from around the globe attended the New York funeral. But it was in Hartford that I said my goodbye to Sophie.

A strong winter wind, wet with a cold, heavy rain, blew away any touch of spring the following Sunday as six hundred people sat in sadness at the second funeral of Sophie Tucker. The large crowd sat in Hartford's Weinstein Mortuary. We were friends and relatives who knew Sophie always thought of Hartford as home. We sat there and heard our own thoughts being put into words.

His voice wavering and suddenly becoming shrill, and with tears clouding his eyes, Rabbi Isadore A. Aaron said, "I'm glad Sophie has come home." As Rabbi Aaron gave the eulogy, the shiny mahogany casket, covered with red roses, stood in front of him. It was closed, but in our minds and memories everyone present could still see the face of the woman who never said no when charity was mentioned or when she was asked to sing.

There were no George Jessels at the Weinstein Mortuary Sunday, just the everyday business people whom Sophie never forgot. People like Joseph Rifkin, who lives at the Thomas Hooker Hotel.

"Look at this," Rifkin said, just before the 1:30 service started. In his right hand he clutched a slightly soiled thank-you card with the name "Sophie Tucker" printed on it. She had sent it to him about two months earlier when he had sent her a card after he heard that she was in the hospital in New York.

"Sophie waited on me in 1906," said a man named Morris Kaufman. "I used to go to Abuza's Restaurant in Hartford. It was her family's place." It was also the place Sophie Tucker started singing for small change as she waited on tables.

In a row near Morris Kaufman sat a man named Mitchell Silversmith, who had come from New Bedford, Massachusetts for the funeral. He said he was a distant relative. "Why aren't they going to bury Sophie at the old Zion Hill Cemetery?" Kaufman asked Silversmith. "I thought they'd bury her with her parents. Why Emanuel Cemetery in Wethersfield?"

"No room," said Silversmith.

And by now there was no more room in the chapel; it was about one o'clock. They had to use other rooms where an intercom piped in the service.

"You know, I saw Sophie in Miami two years ago," Silversmith said. "She went on for two and one-half hours without stopping for a second. Silversmith's wife's lips began to tremble slightly, and she asked her husband for a handkerchief.

Everyone was having a hard time realizing that Sophie wouldn't be singing anymore. When people came into the Farmington Avenue chapel, many were greeted by a tall, thin man with a face lined with age and reddened from crying. It was Moe. Morris Abuza, Brother, Sophie's manager. He presided at this second funeral just as he had at the first one in New York.

At one thirty Cantor Koret's full tenor voice sang the first bars of a psalm which begins, "Lord, what is man?" He sang it in Hebrew, and Rabbi Novack of Emanuel Synagogue translated it. When the cantor began, the sound of people weeping quietly drifted through the chapel.

Rabbi Novack said nice things about Sophie. He said, "We, in Hartford, respected her. We respected the name she made for herself just with her inner determination."

Rabbi Aaron, a friend of Sophie's for years spoke fondly too, "We Jews are told there are only 36 righteous men in each generation. Sophie Tucker belongs in this category. She felt a responsibility for everyone. She felt we were all God's children."

In about forty-five minutes it was over, and they were carrying the casket down a long reddish carpet to the hearse waiting in the rain with scores of mourners.

A little before three o'clock, a few hundred people stood in the drenching rain, which was thrown in their faces by the wind. We stood on the muddy ground at Emanuel Cemetery with the water dripping off the corners of the green canvas canopy that covered Sophie's casket and Bert and Moe. Some of us stood under the canopy, but many people were outside in the rain.

We chanted the *Kaddish*, the Jewish prayer for the dead.

"Receive in mercy the soul of our departed Sophie Tucker," said Rabbi Aaron.

Bert and Moe were bent over in grief, their heads bowed.

It was only the second time that I had been in Bert's presence. I was struck by how small he was, short and slight of build. Nothing like Sophie. I thought that he probably took after his father, Louis Tuck. I tried to recall the day that Sophie had told me stories about Bert, his flirtation with show business, and her guilt about having left him behind when she fled Hartford and went to New York. All that was history now as Sophie and her son were both in Hartford…Sophie under the ground and Bert bent over in grief above that very ground.

Just as the service ended, a husky, light-haired man was crying as he walked past me and lightly touched my arm, then walked to the casket. Aloud he said, "Mom's here, too." He looked down at the ground next to Sophie's casket, shaking his head.

It was Charles. He was standing by Sophie's casket and looking at the grave of his mother, Blanche, who had died two weeks earlier. I was shocked; no one told me.

It hit me then that death was real. It was a hard, final scientific fact. What Sophie was…her hope, her vitality, her love…was gone. I felt an ache. I also felt Sophie's presence strongly.

We miss Sophie...I miss her. Just as the Sophie Tucker legend lives on, so do my rich memories of Cuz Sophie and the great influence she had on my life. She is with me everyday...her words, her lessons and the great love she showered on us, her family.

As she wrote to me in 1960: "Stay close to your own. There is nothing more important than family..."

So I stay close to her, her spirit, her wisdom and the warm memories we shared. Without Sophie I'm empty. In my bones I feel a void, but I carry her in my heart...that's where I have the words of encouragement she always gave to me so freely. So many things that she taught me I will carry to my grave and pass on to my children and to you, those who remember or read the legend who was Sophie Tucker, the Last of the Red Hot Mamas.

# PART TWO

# CHAPTER 23

▼

# MOE IN MAJORCA

*"Some of these days" it had to happen. That great old song rasped out again and again for decades. "Some of These Days," as Sophie Tucker sang it, was an anthem of optimism and with it Sophie steamed up through vaudeville and Broadway to show business immortality...her huge frame shaking and the mutes off her brassy voice. Sophie herself was never wicked but her exuberance and racy songs made people feel wicked without the wear and tear of being so.*

*She was loud and strong, and kept shouting her gospel of good times and goodwill until she died. As Sophie said," Giving is a part of show business. Besides, darling, everybody knows you can't take it with you!"*

Moe Abuza was a different man after Sophie died. In two years time he had lost his wife, his beloved sister and his raison d'être. My parents made it a point to check on Moe weekly and to include him in their social life. My father and Moe had lunch together once a week. Two or three times a month the three of them had dinner together.

Within those two years, Charles met and married Susie, a "shicksa," and within five years they had a son and a daughter. Moe was now a grandfather, a role that helped him move on with his own life. During the final years of his life, with Blanche and Sophie gone, and few means of passing the idle hours, Moe took to traveling.

On a whim and with my father's encouragement, Moe took a trip to the Far East. He was gone for a month. When he returned, he called my father, and they met for lunch.

My father was delighted with how Moe looked...tanned, happy, rested.

"Moe, the trip did wonders for you," Daddy said, as they each ordered a martini.

"You should only know," Moe responded, winking playfully.

"Yeah? What is it?"

"I met someone...a marvelous girl," Moe said. "She's Chinese, beautiful, smart, and she loves me."

"Wait a minute...go slowly. Where did you meet this..."

"Susie, her name is Susie," Moe said, beaming. "And I met her one night when I was having dinner with some old friends in Hong Kong. I thought she was beautiful."

"And? What did she think?"

"She liked me. We saw each other every night that I was in Hong Kong. She's planning to come for a visit in a few months. Meanwhile, I gave her some business advice. She's in retail. I backed her latest business venture," he said, proudly.

"You what? Moe, I once told you to call me before you do anything like that. How much did you put up?" Daddy said, clearly upset.

"Twenty five grand," Moe said. "It's okay. I can afford it."

"Did she sign any papers or anything. Is it a loan?"

"Nah. I trust her. Milt, she loves me. I feel like a million bucks."

"How old is Susie?" Daddy asked.

"Thirty-one. I know, I know...I'm two and a half times her age. Trust me on this one, Milt."

My father leaned forward and lowered his voice. "Did you sleep with her?"

"Of course I did. What? You think I'm too old to still get it up?" Moe said.

"That's not what I'm implying. Bedfellows, however, often make bad business partners. This isn't wise," Daddy said.

"Wise, schmize...it's a done deal. And I've never been happier," Moe said.

Daddy realized that there was no talking any sense into Moe, so he stopped his badgering for the moment. "So...when will I get to meet her?"

"When she comes to New York in a few months. I promise. You and Marion will be our guests for dinner somewhere snazzy. I'll let you know."

Six months later, after many excuses and postponed trips, Susie came to New York and Moe called my parents. They agreed to meet at the Four Seasons for dinner.

Moe and Susie were waiting at a table near the wall when my parents arrived at the restaurant. Moe stood up and held my mother's chair for her.

My father and Moe embraced. My father bent at the waist and offered Susie his hand, which she took in her tiny one.

"So pleased to meet you," my father said.

Susie looked at Moe. "Susie, this here is Milton Young...our lawyer and my cousin. And the pretty one is Marion, Milton's better half," Moe said.

My father sat back in his chair, observing Susie, thinking what a stylish woman she was. She wore a well-cut tailored suit of black wool with black satin lapels and cuffs, and to his seasoned eye it was obviously couture. Her only pieces of jewelry were pearl earrings, a single strand of large South Sea pearls and a platinum watch. Simple, understated, very chic. She had a refined air about her. There was something else, an aloof politeness about her that made him feel uneasy.

My mother immediately sat down in a chair, smiling coolly at Susie.

"When did you get in?" my father asked Susie, trying to make small talk.

Susie looked at Moe who spoke for her. "She arrived three days ago. Susie wants to do some buying for her store in Hong Kong while she's in New York. We shopped for the past two days."

"And what kind of store do you have?" my father asked.

This time when Susie deferred to Moe he encouraged her to speak for herself. "Tell them, Susie. I simply bank-rolled it, but you know more about it than I do."

My mother kicked my father under the table.

"It's a boutique," Susie said, taking a sip of her water. "We sell designer scarves, purses, some clothes. I am thinking about adding jewelry to the inventory."

"Have you ever undertaken such an enterprise before?" my father asked.

"Not something I owned, but I have worked in several Hong Kong boutiques before," Susie responded.

The waiter interrupted the interrogation, much to Susie's relief. Once they had put in their dinner orders, Moe raised his glass in a toast. "To my Susie," he said, nodding at her. "She has made me feel like a young man again."

Susie looked embarrassed. My parents were uncomfortable, but they politely raised their glasses and sipped at their respective drinks.

Throughout most of the meal, Moe lauded many fine qualities of Susie—...her business acumen, her beauty, her kindness to him. Susie said very little.

When I heard about Susie I asked my parents, "Do you think she's a gold-digger?"

My mother laughed sarcastically. "What do you think? What could a young girl like that want from a guy like Moe except his money."

"Now, Marion, don't be nasty. They both can benefit from the relation-ship. Susie gets a sugar daddy, and Moe gets to feel young and sexy. No one necessarily gets hurt, and they both get something they want and need," Daddy said.

Within a year, Moe was talking about moving Susie to New York and helping her open a boutique in Manhattan. He also hinted at marrying her. He bought a condominium on the island of Majorca so that he and Susie had a place to vacation the following year.

It was 1972, six years after Sophie's death. Roy and I were struggling to save our marriage. We had three children now. In 1968 I had given birth to another boy, Billy. My husband and I decided to take a trip, just the two of us. My parents agreed to watch the children while we were away.

After talking to travel agents and poring over travel brochures, we settled on Majorca. My father told us that part of the time that we would be in Majorca, Moe would be there. He gave us Moe's telephone number and address in Majorca, and I promised that we would call him.

I hadn't seen Moe in four years. He sounded thrilled to hear my voice when I telephoned. "Maybe while you're in Majorca," Moe said, "you'll get to meet Susie. She's supposed to be coming in two days to spend the weekend with me. Save Saturday night…the four of us will go out for dinner. Meanwhile, Loey, I can't wait to see you and your husband. Come to my apartment this evening at six o'clock; we'll have a drink, and then I'll take you out to my favorite restaurant for dinner. What do you say?"

We agreed.

The apartment building where Moe owned a condominium was a modern white building shaped like a semi-circle. We rode the elevator to the tenth floor and rang Moe's bell.

No response.

We rang again. Finally, the door opened. Moe flung his big arms around me and planted a wet kiss on my cheek. "Loey, let me look at you." He pushed me away and looked me up and down. "You look good, very good." He shook Roy's hand. "Come in…come in," he said, leading us into a living room stuffed with furniture that was too big for the apartment

"Goddamn it!" he screamed. "Shit!"

We were puzzled. "Are you okay?" I asked.

"It's this damn hearing aid," Moe explained. "I hate it. It has a habit of emitting a high screech for no reason. It hurts my ears! I've taken it in to be fixed many times, but the damn thing persists in torturing me. But—I can't hear without it, so bear with me."

Moe went to the bar set up in one corner of the room. "What can I get you guys to drink?" he asked. He crushed his cigar into an ashtray.

"White wine," Roy and I said in unison.

"You got it!" Moe said, serving each of us a glass.

I was aware of the emptiness in the room, the absence of Sophie who had usually been present when I was with Moe. As if reading my thoughts, Moe said, "Daddy sent me a copy of the article you had published, Loey. Sophie would have been so proud of you."

"Thank you," I said. "I owe it all to Sophie, you know. She's the one who encouraged me to write."

"Goddamn it!" Moe was screaming again. Suddenly he ripped the hearing aid out of his ear and threw it on an end table. "Excuse me," he said, and went into his bedroom.

Fifteen minutes later Moe returned, with a new hearing aid in his ear. "I'm going back to this old hearing aid," he said. "It's not strong enough for me, but it's better than having that thing screech at me."

"Can we help?" I asked.

"What!?" Moe yelled.

He couldn't hear most of what we said as he got his raincoat and yelling directions at us, led us outside. Moe walked with a cane now. With his cane in one hand, and the other hand hooked onto my arm, the three of us walked to the building next door where Moe's favorite restaurant was.

Dinner was a disaster. Moe screamed at the waiters to burn his food more. He spilled wine on the tablecloth when he took a fistful of ice cubes and splashed them into his wineglass. He shouted rather than spoke his words, and heard very little of what Roy said as he tried to carry on a conversation. I was both mortified and sad by Moe's obvious decline.

Most of Moe's conversation at dinner concerned Susie and her impending arrival on the island of Majorca. "The four of us will have a grand time when Susie arrives," Moe promised. "We'll do the town."

By ten o'clock we took Moe back to his apartment, and bid him good night. "I'll call you tomorrow when Susie has unpacked, and we'll make our plans," he promised as he kissed me goodnight, holding his now soggy cigar in one hand.

"Okay, Moe," I said gently. "Get a good night's sleep. We'll talk to you tomorrow."

When Moe hadn't called us the next day I called him at six in the afternoon. "Moe?" I said loudly when he answered the telephone.

"What?" he screamed into the telephone.

"Moe! It's me...Lois!" I yelled.

"Loey...hi, baby. I thought you were Susie," he said.

"How is she?" I asked.

"Meet me at the same restaurant we went to last night. I left word with the concierge to tell Susie when she arrives to come next door for dinner. But the three of us will get a head start. Meet me in twenty minutes," and he hung up.

Roy and I had no choice but to race over to the restaurant and spend another evening with Moe. He was waiting when we arrived, yelling at the waiter to bring him burnt garlic bread and more ice for his wine.

"Oh, boy," Roy whispered to me. "Here we go again."

"I feel sorry for him," I whispered back. "He's lonely."

"What about Susie?" Roy whispered.

"I have a bad feeling about her. I think she going to stand him up," I said.

Moe was delighted to see us. He waved us into our seats. "I think we should go ahead and order. Susie might be very late. The steaks are good...so is the roast beef. What do you guys want to eat?"

We ordered steaks and salad. Moe's steak was burned to a crisp, and his baked potato skin was just as black. He put globs of butter on his potato and waved his fork in the air as he said, "You'll love Susie, I know you will. I don't know what's keeping her." He looked at his watch.

We ate as slowly as we could and ordered dessert with our coffee. Still no Susie. Moe kept his eyes glued to the entrance of the restaurant, searching pathetically for Susie. No Susie. Moe seemed hardly aware that we were in the room at all. At times his mind appeared to drift directionlessly, from one subject to the next, his eyes sometimes fixed in a motionless frieze, sometimes roaming from place to place about the room.

By midnight after two cups of coffee and after Moe had smoked two cigars, Moe pushed his chair away from the table. "Something must have happened to detain her," he said. "Let's go!"

Moe promised to call us the next day. We escorted him back to his apartment and left feeling sorry for him.

When we didn't hear from Moe the following day, Roy and I went to his apartment.

When we knocked on the door it was unlocked and swung open.

"Susie?" Moe called out.

"It's just us!" I called in response. "We were worried about you."

Moe was sitting idly, his hands in his lap, the cane propped up against the wall to his left. He looked up sharply at our entrance, like someone pulled abruptly from a long period of deep concentration, his face cast in a mood of troubled thoughtfulness.

"I am perfectly well, Loey, very much improved, and thank you for asking," Moe said, looking across at me and smiling.

I smiled back, and there was both warmth and affection in my voice when I asked, "Did you hear from Susie?"

He nodded. "She's not coming."

I was about to ask him what happened when there was a tap on the door, and the concierge entered. "The locksmith will be here in an hour," he said.

"Thank you, Bob," Moe said.

Taking a puff of his cigar, Moe glanced at me surreptitiously. "I'm having the locks changed on my door. I'll be damned if that tramp will ever have access to this place again."

The phone suddenly rang and Moe lifted the receiver. "Yes," he yelled. There was a pause as he listened and then he said, "Oh, all right, put her on."

As Moe listened to someone on the other end of the telephone, Roy and I turned our heads away and admired the framed photographs of Sophie that graced a corner table.

Moe finished his phone conversation, hung up, and relit his cigar. "Well, that's that!" he boomed.

"What is it, Moe? Anything wrong?" Roy asked.

Moe sat up ramrod straight in the chair, and there was a faint tinge of white around his mouth, as if the skin were bleached. I knew this was a sign of his anger.

After a moment, he said in a controlled voice, "I simply don't understand. Why would she lie to me? It's preposterous." His brows drew together, knitted in a frown. He shook his head. "I'm a fool. I'm glad Sophie isn't here to see what a fool her brother has been. But it's over. I'll get over her. I have exaggerated Susie's importance, blown her out of all proportion."

I felt great empathy for Moe. I glanced at him and saw the stricken expression in his eyes. My heart went out to him.

Moe, aware of my scrutiny, drew himself up on his chair and said, "So, you guys are leaving in the morning. I guess this is goodbye, then." Then he grasped his cane, edged himself off the chair, and walked to one of the windows that looked out into the harbor.

We didn't stay very long, sensing that Moe wanted to be alone.

When we got to my parents' house to pick up the children, I relayed the Moe/Susie saga to my father.

"Poor guy. I smelled something fishy from the beginning," he said.

"Well, she broke his heart, Daddy," I said. "I feel so sorry for Moe."

"He'll recover, sweetheart. Hopefully, he won't get himself tied up with a gold-digger again."

But Moe never did fully recover. He returned to New York the following week and, within a month, was hospitalized after he suffered a stroke.

The day Moe died I wept for him. He had died a broken man with a broken heart and broken memories. As we sat in the Weinstein Mortuary in Hartford Connecticut to say goodbye to Moe, and later at the cemetery where Moe was buried near Blanche and beside Sophie, I wept some more. It was the end of an era.

It was also the beginning of the end of my marriage to Roy. By 1975, we were separated and the following year divorced.

# CHAPTER 24

▼

# A PLACE CALLED HOME

*"My audience used to like to laugh…now of the songs they want to hear most is, 'There's So Much To Do and So Little Time.' If you go out and ask hundreds of kids what Sophie was talking about, most of them will not know.*

Climbing the front steps, I crossed the porch to knock softly on the old wood door. After a minute's wait, I gave another knock. I was about to go around to the back, when the door opened. I was in Hartford, knocking on the door of the house where Sophie's family last lived. It is a narrow street. Row houses lined both sides of the street. In between every two housing units was a narrow driveway.

"May I help you?" asked a man in his sixties, wearing an undershirt, bald headed and hungry looking.

I extended my right hand. "My name is Lois Young," I said. "I am doing some research on Sophie Tucker, and I understand that her family lived in this house."

The man stared at me blankly. "And?"

"And I wonder if you have any information that would be helpful to me…about Sophie's family and their life here."

He shook his head. "I don't know nothin,'" he said, closing the door.

I walked down the front steps and stood in the driveway. An old woman stood on the sidewalk outside of the house next door. "Did I hear you say Sophie Tucker?" she asked.

"Yes…you did," I said, walking towards her. She was at least eighty-five years old, her thin hair white and partially hidden by a torn scarf. "Did you know her or her family?"

"I knew them all," she said. "They were so proud of Sophie. I remember when she came home to visit. Her parents were bursting with pride, and the whole neighborhood came over to meet her. I can still see it." She paused, as if recalling something. "Sophie's mother was a good woman…very charitable. I've lived next door for more than sixty years, so I saw it all."

I took a note pad out of my purse and was ready to take notes.

"They were good neighbors. A wonderful family," she continued.

"Did you ever meet Sophie Tucker?" I asked, wanting to keep her attention when I saw her eyes wander and her attention wane.

"Many times. I was very upset when I heard that she died. By then the family had sold this house, and I had new neighbors…several times. The people who live there now are unfriendly. Nothing like Sophie's family," she continued.

I feared that I would not get her back to talking about the past she was so intent on voicing her complaints about the present state of the neighborhood. "I'm one of the last remaining old timers who still lives in the old neighborhood. I stay to myself, these days," she continued.

"Did the neighbors around come to see Sophie when she came back to visit as a star? I asked, hoping to learn more about Sophie's home visits.

"They were all mad at her 'cause she left her little boy and ran off. They thought she was a hussy, and everyone was down on her. The neighbors didn't forgive Sophie Tucker for going away, leaving her child and her family. They said only a bad woman would do such a thing."

"They said things like that?" I said.

She nodded. "But Sophie was brazen when she realized how the neighbors felt. She was determined to make the neighbors speak to her, but they turned their backs. Some of the kids would run after her yelling, 'Look, she's got paint on her face. She's no good.' Some of them children pointed their fingers at that little boy and said that his mother was a bad woman who ran away and left him. Sophie's mama was a good woman. She had lots of friends. She'd go door to door collecting pennies, nickels, dimes, quarters, whatever she could get to donate to charity. They were Jewish, you know. One time a bunch of Sophie's mother Jennie's friends went to Poli's to see Sophie's act. Then they acted a little different. All of them more or less complimented Sophie. Not too much…it's the Jewish way to be cautious about compliments…but enough to seem more polite. Whenever Sophie came home she was in no danger of getting a swelled head. The neighborhood made sure of that."

"Did they ever forgive her? For leaving?" I asked, not wanting our conversation to end.

"I guess they did. My family liked her. We never passed judgment. Show business made her rich and she was always good to her family…sent them money, bought her mother fine clothes and jewelry. But leaving her little boy was not a good thing. She sent money to take care of him, too. But he was spoiled rotten. Sophie's little sister, Annie, was like a mother to that boy. Sophie made enough money to send that boy away to boarding school. I wonder how he turned out? Do you know?"

I nodded. "Bert was okay. He married and was close to his mother, but he died pretty young, after Sophie died. A heart attack. He never had any children of his own," I said.

She shook her head. "Tssk, tssk. What a shame. She never should have left him so young. It probably broke his heart or damaged it in some way. That's why he's dead today," she said.

"I think they made peace with each other," I said, feeling defensive about Sophie's motherhood.

"Maybe…but you can't make up for those early years when a boy needs his mother to take care of him."

I wasn't about to explain how guilty Sophie always felt about having left Bert, or about the strain between them. Instead, I turned around and snapped several photographs of the Abuza house and two photographs of the old woman before I climbed back into my car and drove away.

I was in Hartford trying to visit some of Sophie's old haunts. I hadn't had much luck, however, since many of the landmarks had been torn down and parking lots or modern sky scrapers had replaced the old family restaurant, the gas station where Louis Tuck had worked when he and Sophie were falling in love, and the Brown School where the Abuza children had been educated.

That night, I dreamed I had gone back to the old house and met Sophie's parents. They were a miniature version of the family pictures I had seen. They knew exactly who I was. Parental pride swelled so that Sophie's parents grew a whole twelve inches, there and then, in my dream.

I awoke with a start, feeling the sadness of knowing that the dream was only a dream. There was no going back. The past was dead, and I had to invent it from the photographs and memories available to me.

# PART THREE

# CHAPTER 25

▼

# TRIFLES AND TREASURES

*Mention must be made of Ted Shapiro, the Red Hot Mamma's accompanist for forty-three years. Starting in 1922, Shapiro accompanied Sophie Tucker for virtually all of her records, radio, television, film, and variety appearances around the world. Ted often collaborated with Jack Yellen and others on Sophie Tucker's special material. His song "If I Had You" became a standard. Shapiro's work with Tucker during the Jazz Age ranged from a solo piano backing on the great ballad "The One I Love" to a virtual duet on a characteristic comedy item "I Don't Want To Get Thin," performed in Sophie Tucker's feature film "Honky Tonk."*

I kept my promise to Sophie and after earning my undergraduate degree I went on to study creative writing and earned my masters of Arts degree. My writing career has included teaching writing at various colleges and many published articles, stories and a book of poetry, but my most important piece of writing is the one about Sophie and me. I have been gathering information, recalling the past and corresponding with and interviewing people relevant to this story.

On August 7, 1987, twenty years after Sophie's death, I received a note from Susan Shapiro, the widow of Ted Shapiro. She had heard that I was attempting to write a book about Sophie Tucker.

*Good luck with your venture. I have Sophie's picture in my store, and you'd be amazed at the number of people who ask about her. I've been told by customers that they've gone to the library to find something about Sophie's life, but there's nothing available.*

Susan Shapiro's note was followed by her letter:

*Dear Dr. Young,*

*Received your letter of July 13th. I would be happy to help you if you are going to write something meaningful and true and not unkind. Another relative of Sophie's approached me and I was going to help her, but she sent me a script to read that made me so angry that I want nothing to do with her. It was all about what a homely fat child she was and when she first performed for the public, they would only let her sing black face because she was so homely. It went on to say what a terrible mother she was and how her son hated her. The whole thing was a character assassination and there wasn't one word about the good she did; not even one scene recalling her fabulous nightclub acts. I don't think the world needs another book like "Mommy Dearest." There is some sadness in every life, and you can touch on that, but it should be done in a way that people are moved to be compassionate and understanding. The public loved Sophie. They loved the way she was on stage, and I don't want to see her destroyed.*

*We loved her and understood her. A lot of her gruffness that some people complained about was shyness. I remember when I married Teddy; we were going to have a reception and Sophie insisted on going with me to buy a dress for the occasion. I was not really thrilled about the idea, but I did it because I did not marry Teddy to make problems in his working relationship. Luckily the dress that Sophie insisted I buy was also my choice so the shopping was not as painful as I feared it might be. After we bought the dress, Sophie wanted to go on shopping, and we did. The dress had been really more than I wanted to spend because I sew, and I knew within one dollar what I could have made the dress for, but it was a once in a lifetime occasion. I did think silently that after I had the shoes dyed to match (a custom in those years) I was through shopping for the day. Sophie wanted to shop jewelry and handbags, etc.*

*I took her and went along, but it is not my nature to give my opinion unless asked, and I did not hang over Sophie's shoulder when she was buying, but passed the time looking in the cases.*

*After the shopping, I took Sophie to rehearse with Teddy. About 4:30 when they took a break, I called up to the stage to Teddy that I was leaving and would he take Sophie home. Sophie called out in her manner, saying, "Don't forget to put my packages in Teddy's car."*

*When Teddy came in, about six o'clock, he was carrying Sophie's packages. I said, "Oh, Teddy, didn't you hear Sophie say she wanted her packages in your car?"*

*He laughed and said, "They're from Sophie to you."*

*I opened the package to find the bag Sophie thought I should have with my dress and pearl earrings to match the string of pears Teddy had given me. Well, of course, I rushed right to the phone to call Sophie and thank her, but before I could even get all the words out Sophie said, "It's nothing at all, nothing at all," and she hung up.*

*That's what strangers didn't understand. She wanted to be loved, but she was often too shy to accept it, except on stage or with people she had grown to trust (and that took a long time).*

*Teddy loved Sophie. You don't stay fifty years with someone you don't care for. He had other job offers, but he never would have left her, even when they fought and sometimes they did, she was so childlike.*

*One time, Teddy found a peacock dish made in colors with luster where the tail fanned out. Teddy showed it to Sophie, bragging about his find. Sophie took a fancy to it, and wanted it. He loved it, and didn't want to part with it. She (Sophie) didn't speak directly to Teddy for about two weeks. She could be standing next to him, and she would say to a third party present, "Tell Teddy this or tell Teddy that."*

*I kept saying, "Teddy, it's only a dish, give it to her."*

*Finally, he did, and she started speaking to him directly from that moment on, and it was never mentioned again!*

*I find writing very tiresome since I had my stroke, though I am completely recovered except I can't remember numbers and spelling now throws me. But I run a business and nobody notices.*

*I will answer any questions you want to ask me if your book is not destructive.*

*Sincerely,*
*Susan Shapiro*

Susan Shapiro's letter tells us something about Sophie's relationship with Ted Shapiro. After I read it several times, I put it in the large cardboard box that held my scribbled notes and photographs of Sophie and labeled the box *Sophie and Me*. And there it sat with everything else while my own life was in turmoil.

Nineteen eighty-seven was a busy year because it was that year when I married my second husband. David was born and raised in Hartford, Connecticut, Sophie's hometown. Coincidentally, his grandparents and mother had all died at the Jewish Home for the Aged, the very place that Sophie's mother helped start and that Sophie herself financed and help expand into one of the finest old age homes in the state.

I tabled *Sophie and Me* for about seven years until 1994. When my brother-in-law George's mother died on Monday, June 13, 1994, David and I drove up to Hartford for the funeral.

When we entered Weinstein Mortuary I realized that Sophie had been brought there from New York for her second funeral and burial. As we entered the mortuary, I noticed the three proprietors at the entry; there were two older men and a younger one. Before the service started I approached the oldest man.

"Excuse, me. As I recall, Sophie Tucker's funeral took place here, didn't it," I asked.

He smiled and said, "Yes. I took care of Sophie. I took care of the whole family."

I shared with him my relationship to Sophie and my interest in learning as much as possible about her life in Hartford.

"Wait here," he said. He ducked into an office and disappeared for several minutes. He reappeared before the service that I was to attend began and handed me two pieces of paper. Written on one piece was *Henry Abuza, 271 South Street, Vernon, CT* and a telephone number. The other was a photocopy of a page taken from a publication called *Hartford Jews 1659-1970*.

Later, as David and I drove back to David's sister's house to sit *shiva* with his family, I read the article which was a write-up of Sophie's parents Charles P. and Jennie Abuza followed by information about Phillip Abuza, Sophie's older brother. I folded up the two papers and tucked them into my purse. I planned to call Henry Abuza, Brother Phillip's son, when I was back home in Philadelphia.

On Wednesday, June 15, 1994, I called Henry Abuza's house. A man answered the telephone.

"Is Henry Abuza there?" I asked.

"This is he," he said. "Yes?" His voice was strong yet gentle, educated but unaffected, warm and friendly.

I explained who I was, mentioning both the book I wanted to write about Sophie and me and also mentioning our familial connection.

"I remember the name Yanowich and they were relatives," he said. (Yanowich was my father's birth name.)

I told Henry that I was interested in knowing about Sophie and Phillip's working relationship and anything else he could tell me.

Henry hesitated a moment. A little stiffly he said, "Phillip Abuza was my father and Sophie's business manager. He was the oldest of the four children...the birth order was Phillip, Sophie, Moe and then Annie. My father was Sophie's business manager, and he was devoted to her interests. Sophie made a lot of money. She enjoyed money but couldn't hold on to it. My father was afraid that something would happen…Sophie might lose her voice or popularity one day and he felt that he had to make Sophie toe the line with finances so she had a nest egg for her future. At one time I had all of my father's documents on Sophie's finances as well as every letter she wrote to him, but," and Henry paused. "But, when my father died and the family split I got rid of everything."

"The family split?" I asked. It was the first time I had heard of it.

"My father died in 1945," Henry said.

That's why I never met him, I thought. I didn't meet Sophie until the 1950s. "Go on," I urged Henry.

"My father's funeral was on a Friday. The following Monday the headline in the Hartford paper was *Sophie Tucker Sues Brother's Wife For Half a Million Dollars*. I'm 83 years old, Lois, and I remember it like it was yesterday. At the time I was married to my first wife. My mother lived in the south end of Hartford. None of us had even been told by Sophie or by Moe that my mother was being sued and, worse, because she was being accused of making a grab for Sophie's money. Annie and I were always close. I called Annie when I read the newspaper headline but Annie said that there was nothing to talk about. She told me to turn over everything to Sophie, as if I was helping my mother hide Sophie's money. I guess Annie's own financial dependency on Sophie made her too scared to talk to me about it."

I was silent. It was the first I had heard of any of this.

"For two years we endured conflict and litigation. And that because of Sophie's expecting everyone to cater to her. I remember that when Sophie came to New York she'd check into a big hotel suite and the whole family was supposed to come and pay court to her. But she didn't even stop playing cards when we showed up. She'd ignore us because she was embroiled in her card game. It was usually pinochle. Her piano player, Ted Shapiro, made twice as much playing cards with Sophie than he made in salary. A good part of the family was dependent on Sophie's generosity for their livelihood. Sophie bought her mother a house. She supported her parents. She supported Annie and Jules. Moe, Annie, even Charles never tried to make peace with our side of the family. Instead, they latched onto what Sophie had."

Henry was on a roll now. He didn't need me to say anything because he was getting a lot off of his chest.

He went on, "Sophie was like her father Charlie. He would sit in his restaurant all day and play cards, but he played very well, Sophie loved her cards, and she'd play for money. I remember my father blowing up when Sophie lost $15,000 one night playing cards with L.B. Mayer."

Henry was silent for several minutes. "Henry, are you still there?" I asked.

"I am. Raking up old coals is getting to me, though. I hope you've learned something from what I've told you," he said.

"Yes….I'd like to talk with you more some other time," I said.

"You say you're a writer. Have you had anything published that I can see?" he asked.

"I recently had a book of my poetry published. I'll send you a copy," I promised.

"On my refrigerator I have a Louis Ginsberg quote that says something like 'The only thing you have in life is what you give away.' I would love it if you gave me a copy of your book."

"Next time in Hartford…my husband's family lives there…I will call you. Maybe we can get together in person," I said.

"I'd like that," Henry said.

I sent Henry a copy of my book and got the following reply:

*July 3, 1994*

*Dear Lois,*

*It was very lovely of you to send me a copy of "Escape Roots." I have enjoyed reading it. I hope we can meet when next you are in this area. Please let Florence and I know when you will be in the Hartford area so that we can make a good effort to meet!*

*Regards,*
*Henry*

Enclosed was the following quote attached to a note that said, "This is the simple couplet I was trying to quote to you:
*Love that is hoarded moulds at last*
*Until we know some day*
*The only thing we ever have*
*Is what we give away.*
*Louis Ginsberg, Poet, Educator (1896-1977)*

On August 19, 1994, David and I drove to West Hartford, Connecticut and were the guests of Henry and his wife Florence Abuza at their country club. With his permission, I tape recorded our conversation. The transcript of that conversation follows.

## Transcript of Henry Abuza's comments

### August 19, 1994
### West Hartford, CT
### Dinner at country club with Henry and Florence Abuza

"It's possible that my mother and Sophie were childhood friends, but I don't think so. I know Sophie always said so, but a lot of things that Sophie said were exaggerations. Any kind of publicity was good for her; she did a very good job. She kept books with the names of people with whom she kept in touch. In that sense she was good. She was terrible with money. She would never have enough money at the end of a year to pay her taxes. That's why my father, Sophie's older brother, became her manager. My father was devoted to her. They were very close. I was too young to remember everything, but I do remember that my father put Sophie's concerns ahead of my mother's. It ran in the family. After my father died, Moe did the same thing and put Sophie's concerns ahead of Blanche's.

"Sophie's relationship with you, Lois, was another side of her. But when we came to New York to see her whenever she took a suite of rooms in a hotel she wasn't very nice. Everybody in the family would come because the family meant a lot to her. But she would be playing cards, pinochle. We'd come in and Sophie would say, 'Hello, darling,' and she'd put her face up for me to kiss. Then we were supposed to just sit while she played cards. This would happen even when I was already in my twenties. But, before that, when I was younger, Sophie would come to our house. My father was the oldest child and, therefore, the head of the family. All the holidays and Seders were in our house. I remember my grandmother Jenny but not my grandfather Charles. Moe's son's name was Charles after our grandfather. When my father died, the family became estranged. The only one to call me over the years was Moe's son Charles. Charles had a son and he was like Charles, not the greatest student. Anyway, he called because he wanted to know if I could get his son into Trinity College. My first wife's brother was a lifetime trustee of Trinity. So I did it, and Charles' son got in. And that was the last I heard from Charles. He's dead, you know. Died of a heart attack before he was sixty.

"Now Sophie's son Bert. He married Lillian, and they didn't have children. My mother and Annie raised Bert. Bert was in our house a lot. My mother took care of him a lot. Sophie was busy with her career. She was single minded and devoted to her career. She tried at different times to do things for Bert. She sent him to military school.

"My father was the dictator of the whole crew when he was alive. He was the boss. I used to have all the letters that Sophie wrote to him. One night she played pinochle with LB Mayer and lost $15,000. For Sophie to lose $15,000 in one night, and that was a long time ago...that would be like $50,000 today. There was no reason for her to be playing for those stakes. She begged my father for forgiveness and for the money. My father was worried and upset that Sophie would lose her source of income. Lord knows that Sophie had the ability to spend it. He worried that she'd be poor. He wasn't worried about my mother as much, but that's another story.

"So Sophie wrote this letter apologizing and asking my father to forgive her, she'd never do it again. The whole thing is so distasteful. When my father died and Sophie sued my mother was a bitter time. My father died on a Friday and on Monday the headlines read that Sophie Sues Sister-In-Law For Half A Million Dollars. While there was pending litigation, my mother was left for two and a half years not knowing if she would have a pot to pee in or not. We finally agreed that we would put everything, all the records and information that we had, into the hands of an accountant. We'd abide by whatever the accountant decided.

"Meanwhile, Sophie, through her attorney, said if we turned everything over to her, in exchange she would take care of my mother, Leah. My mother couldn't bear that. She had lived as a second class citizen because of Sophie throughout her marriage to my father. Our attorney said that we didn't want anything of Sophie's, all we wanted was what's Leah's. My mother didn't want to be a ward of Sophie like the rest of the family; that was anathema for my mother. She had lived on hand-me-downs from Sophie and what the hell did she want to continue that for. It took two years to settle. The accountant said that they had examined the records and their conclusion was that my father had no resources of his own, and that everything was Sophie's. That was kind of a shock.

"I asked them to take the trouble to lead me through this thing. And you know what, they couldn't substantiate it. There were no clear funds that were solely my father's from any business that had been his. He had taken over the garage of Sophie's husband Frank Wesphal who didn't know the front end of a car from the back end of a car. In all her wisdom, Sophie bought Frank a garage, and Frank would go back and forth to a club gambling. People would put their car in that garage, and the garage would be closed up Thursday to Monday. My father saved it by taking over the garage. He managed Sophie's assets and affairs so he took over the garage. He also paid her back for all the money she invested in the garage. He then took a bankrupt garage, and turned it around and made it the best garage in the town of Baldwin, Long Island, so those resources should have been attributed to my father not to Sophie.

"Then we were faced with, if I remember correctly, legal and accounting fees because of Sophie's law suit against us. We had accrued debt of something like forty grand. Here was my mother on hold financially for two years, a widow. Should we encourage her to seek another law firm and do the whole thing over again?

"Since the time my father died, I never spoke to Sophie. And Annie was a disappointment. Halpern was the lawyer who encouraged Sophie to do this to us. He's a significant person in what happened. The instigator. Halpern and my father had been very close, too. Halpern was a real estate specialist and had a marriage that went on the rocks. My father wasn't that happily married either. Halpern separated from his family and lived in a New York hotel. Every time my father journeyed to New York he stayed at the same hotel. And this guy dared, without sitting down and talking to us, to vilify my mother in the papers.

"Moe became Sophie's manager after my father died. He had no choice; neither my brother nor I were interested. Moe was a T.L. (touchie licker) That's all he ever was in his life. He never earned a living. He was disbarred from his first law case.

"I'll tell you a little drama. My father was laid to rest in the cemetery, and we went back afterwards to my mother's house. Sophie was there, too. We were standing in the back bedroom and the most upset person was Sophie. It was Sophie, in that room, and my brother Zack, Mo, Annie and myself. Sophie was wringing her hands and moaning, 'What'll I do, what'll I do!' Moe was right there. Sophie turns to Zack and me and asks us if we'll take charge of her affairs. Moe was there. Sophie didn't even think of him. I was 34 years old then. Moe stood there quietly. He said nothing. Sophie's crying what is she going to do and asks us.

"Sophie and Moe looked alike. I look like my mother, nothing like Sophie. My father looked like Sophie and Moe. Annie looked like her mother. Sure, over the years, Sophie was generous with money but she had needs. Her needs were all encompassing. I guess I never got caught up in it. As a youngster there were certain exotic things about having an aunt like Sophie Tucker and going back stage and seeing her in the theater and looking out through the curtains at the Palace Theater and seeing 3500 people, and she could turn them on and she could turn them off. Wow! She was, in that respect, remarkable. She could control the audience. She'd cry. She could cry on cue. She could mean it, too.

"Her son Bert was a little guy…built like a jockey. Sophie was a warm Jewish Mama who was cold hearted about her career and left her son…a life of contradictions. There were a lot of long years of bitterness. I never did get to see Annie. She died after Sophie. I lost a whole side of my family. My mother was destroyed. Bert probably died of venereal disease. He was bitter and a wise guy, too.

"Sophie left me $5,000 when she died. I don't know why. She didn't leave any money to my brother or sister. My father had three children and only one, me, received money. I felt guilty about this. I got five grand in her will. I can't figure that out. I never told my brother or sister about the money. I still to this day don't know why the hell she did it...why me? On the other hand, my sister Sadie never married, and the highlight of her life was when she traveled with Sophie.

"If Bert were alive today he'd be in his eighties, but he was never healthy. Bert Tucker. He was never nice to his wife Lillian. This guy should have been a ward of the state...a real creep. He lived in New York. Sophie supported him. He took her money and ran. She felt guilty about Bert her whole life."

# PART FOUR

# CHAPTER 26

▼

# LETTERS FROM SOPHIE
# AND
# PHOTOGRAPHS

Photographs are wonderful things. They capture moments that would otherwise be lost and save them for all time. A photograph can come alive to capture a world of emotions. With time, I have adjusted to the idea that what remains of Sophie is her pure spirit. That doesn't mean I have stopped missing her. She is an irrevocable part of who I am. Sophie believed that anything was possible. I like to think it is. Sophie's life touched on our beliefs about family as it relates to hopes and dreams. Her life was about being an optimist, about being imaginative, about having an open mind. She was a generous and charitable woman who serves as a role model for my family. Though she's been dead now for more than thirty years, she lives on. Sophie was about fighting for what we want in

life, about redefining our everyday lives to return the spark and spontane-
ity that too often get lost in the shuffle.

This section contains letters and postal cards that Sophie sent to me;
letters and postal cards that Sophie sent to Linda Shaw (Janet's sister); several newspaper clippings about Sophie, photographs of the family
reunion, some of Sophie's visits to my parents' home and photographs
from Sophie's own photo album.

These last pages document the years when Sophie acted as my mentor,
my friend, my relative.

## Sophie Tucker Letter Transcribed
### May 31, 1952
### To the Author's father when his father died.

Dear Milton,

Mo just wrote me about your Dad's passing on.

Ann and I send you our heart felt sympathy and
to the rest of the family.

We are fine and send love to your Marion and family.

Your
Sophie

## Sophie Tucker Letter Transcribed
**September 21, 1953, written from Sophie Tucker's Park Avenue
Apartment
To "Little" Aunt Sophie and her family**


Dear Sophie & family,

I do hope your children will be able to bring you up
to see me at the Latin Quarter.

I open September 24th for 4 weeks.

Love to all,

Sophie

## Sophie Tucker Letter Transcribed
### August 24, 1954
### To the Author's cousin (Janet Shaw's sister) Linda Shaw
### While she was at Camp Merrick in Long Island
### Sophie Tucker wrote it from the Fairmont Hotel
### In San Francisco

August 24, 1954

Dear Linda,

So nice hearing from you and you are having such a
nice summer at camp.

I am fine, working hard and loafing between dates
and enjoying my tour out here.

Be sure to give your folks my love, also Grandma Sophie.

Love to you
Yours truly, Cousin Sophie Tucker

## Sophie Tucker Letter Transcribed
### November 20, 1954
### To the Author's cousin (Janet Shaw's sister) Linda Shaw
### in Long Island
### Sophie Tucker wrote it from the The Chase
### In Saint Louis, Missouri


November 20, 1954

Dear Linda,

Nice hearing from you and that you and family and GrandMa are
All well.

Funny I'm expecting a phone call from Milton Young (Author's Father) as
he is in New Orleans and is trying to stop here to see me.

Nice to read of your activities and you do keep busy, which is
fine.

Keep well. Working hard and happy.
I will have my Xmas

Page 2

in Las Vegas this year. My family all keep
fine and I am grateful.

All good wishes to you and family and
my love to all.

Yours truly,
Sophie
Tucker

## Sophie Tucker Letter Transcribed
### February 7, 1955
### To the Author's cousin (Janet Shaw's sister) Linda Shaw
### in Long Island
### Sophie Tucker wrote it from the The Roney Plaza
### In Miami Beach, Florida

February 7, 1955

Dear Linda,

So nice to hear from you and your
various activities while on vacation.

Glad to hear GrandMa and your folks are
all well too.

Page 2

I keep fine. Just arrived here from Las Vegas
and will be here until end of March
and home for Easter.

Have fun.

Love and regards to your GrandMa
and folks.

Yours
Cuz Sophie
Tucker

## Sophie Tucker Letter Transcribed
### January 3, 1956
### To the Shaw Family
### in Long Island
### Sophie Tucker wrote it from the El Rancho Vegas
### In Las Vegas, Nevada
### The card had Sophie's photo on front
### And the inside said:

### December 23$^{rd}$ thru February 7$^{th}$
### Le Roy Prinz Presents
### The Magnificent
### SOPHIE TUCKER
### With
### Ted Shapiro

### Mercury Recording Star
### Guy Cherney
### Ted Fio Rito & His Orchestra

January 3, 1956

A Happy New Year and Love to you all

Sophie
Tucker

## Sophie Tucker Letter Transcribed
### October 26, 1956
### To the Author's cousin (Janet Shaw's sister)

Dear Linda,

Enjoyed your letter very much and good luck to you in your play.

One must start even if it is 12 lines, then you go on and on!

I'm sure your folks will select the right college for you and it's
up to you to work hard and show your folks you mean to do good
so they

p.2
can be proud of you.

I will open at The Town & Country Club in
Brooklyn November 9th for 2 weeks.

Will be wonderful to see the whole family there.

Give my love to Grandma ("Little" Sophie) and for all.

Love,
Sophie
Tucker

## Sophie Tucker Letter Transcribed
### June 23, 1958
### To the Author's cousin (Janet Shaw's sister) Linda Shaw
### in Long Island
### Sophie Tucker wrote it from her Park Avenue Apartment

June 23, 1958

Dear Linda,

Swell hearing from you and your enjoyed
school so much.

Thanks for GrandMa's new address.

I'm fine, resting a few weeks and
off again.

All good wishes to you

Love
Cuz Sophie
Tucker

## Sophie Tucker Letter Transcribed
### July 21, 1958
### To the Author's cousin (Janet Shaw's sister) Linda Shaw
### in Long Island
### Sophie Tucker wrote it from her Park Avenue Apartment

July 21, 1958

Dear Linda,

I just got home from Canadian tour and
off to Pittsburgh now.

Do give your folks my best wishes
for many more Happy Anniversaries.

So glad you are enjoying camp…I keep
fine.

No plans for rest.

Enjoy your summer
Love to you and family

Cuz Sophie
Tucker

## Sophie Tucker Postal Card Transcribed
### October 20, 1959
### To the Author when she was in College
### Letterhead from Palmer House Hotel in Chicago


Dear Lois,

Swell hearing from you. I don't play
Pittsburgh until next June 1960.

I'm fine big success here.

Love and a Happy New Year to
you and Janet.

Love Cuz Sophie Tucker

## Sophie Tucker Postal Card Transcribed
### February 24, 1960
### To the Author when she was in College
### Letterhead from Las Vegas Hotel showing
### On it:

**Stan Irwin Proudly Presents**
**SOPHIE TUCKER**
**Ted Shapiro at the Piano**
**PAUL ANKA**
**In His Premier Night Club Appearance**

Dear Lois

So glad to hear from you and all's well. Wonderful
to hear you're going to
Europe.

I will be home end of March. No plans to play PA at all.

I'm fine.

Love to you and folks.

Cuz Sophie

## Sophie Tucker Letter Transcribed
### March 29, 1960
### To the Author when she was in College
### Letterhead from Tucker Park Avenue Apartment


Dear Lois

Happy to find your letter.

I'm going up to Los Angeles for Pesach. Will be
home April 13. Glad you are enjoying school.

I'm fine only tired.

Love to you dear and folks.

Cuz Sophie

## Sophie Tucker Postal Card Transcribed
### September 20, 1960
### To the Author's cousin (Janet Shaw's sister) Linda Shaw
### in Long Island
### Sophie Tucker wrote it from her Park Avenue Apartment

September 20, 1960

Dear Linda,

Loved hearing from you and family and GrandMa
all are well.

I'm fine.
A Happy New Year and love to you.

## Sophie Tucker Postal Card Transcribed
### October 1960
### To the Author's cousin (Janet Shaw's sister) Linda Shaw
### in Long Island
### Sophie Tucker wrote it from her Park Avenue Apartment
### As a Jewish New Year Card

Dear Linda and Soloman,

Happy to hear you both are well and
happy in your work and family all okay too.

Love,
Cuz Sophie

## Sophie Tucker Letter Transcribed
### February 11, 1961
### To the Author when she was in College
### Letterhead from Deauville Hotel in Miami Beach

February 11, 1961

Dear Lois

So happy to hear from you and family all O.K.

Can't tell you how sorry I am that I won't be at your wedding.
I know you will make a lovely bride and Roy is a fine lad too.

I wish you both long life and happiness.

California is a fine place to live if Roy will be entered in a California
School. Just don't be too far away from your family and don't get
excited about new people, especially away from your own.

L.A. is a tough city and its people are tough too. So use
your good common sense.

I'm fine, off to New Orleans for 2 weeks, Dallas 2 weeks and
home for Easter.

Love to you, Roy and family.

Cuz Sophie

## Sophie Tucker Postal Card Transcribed
### January 24, 1962
### To the Author's cousin (Janet Shaw's sister) Linda Shaw
### in Rochester, New York
### Sophie Tucker wrote it from The Blue Room of The Roosevelt
### In New Orleans, Louisanna


Dear Linda,

Thanks so much for your newsy
letter and I'm glad family and
Grandma all are well.

I'm not sure where I will be June 17, but
I will be in touch with you.

Love,
Cuz Sophie Tucker

## Sophie Tucker Postal Card Transcribed
### August 10, 1965
### To the Author's cousin (Janet Shaw's sister) Linda Shaw
### & her husband S. Solomon
### in Seattle, Washington
### Sophie Tucker wrote it from her Park Avenue Apartment

August 10, 1965

Dear Linda & Solomon.

So nice to get your card and wish you
lots of happiness and good luck in all you
plan to do.

I'm fine.

Love,
Sophie Tucker

## Sophie Tucker Letter Transcribed
### October 5, 1965
### On the birth of Author's second child, son Daniel
### Letterhead from Tucker Park Ave. apartment

October 5, 1965

Dear Lois & Roy -

Mazeltoff and I hope you all are 100% O.K.

Just got back from L.A. to do the Sullivan Show and I am tired out.

Sending a little gift for Daniel.

Keep well.

Love,
Sophie

# Sophie Tucker's Christmas Card
# From Xmas 1965

Dear Children
Happy to
hear from you
and that you
are both doing
so well.
I am coming
along nicely
after my long
seige.
Stay well
love to you both.
Aunt Sophie

Just adding
a little note
to your
Christmas Cheer—
MERRY CHRISTMAS
and
HAPPY NEW YEAR

Love
Sophie
Tucker

## Sophie Tucker's Christmas Card
## From Xmas 1966 When Sophie was Ill

Dear Children

Happy to hear from you and that you are both doing so well.

I'm coming along nicely after my long seige.

Stay well

Love to you both.


Aunt Sophie


(This obviously is written in someone else's handwriting, and Sophie Tucker dictated it to them; however, the card part had her own signature "Love, Sophie Tucker."

# PHOTOGRAPHS
# FROM
# THE
# SOPHIE TUCKER
# FAMILY REUNION
# AT
# AUTHOR'S PARENTS' HOME
# IN
# MOUNT VERNON, NEW YORK

Strand Theatre
Ushers

Lois Young    Milton Young    Marion Young    Mom Young

To the Three dear and Wonderful Youngs—
with sincerest affection—"Mom"

Sophie's parents' last home in Hartford

Sophie's parents' last home in Hartford

The Magnificent
SOPHIE TUCKER

Love Cuz Sophie Tucker

# PHOTOGRAPHS
# FROM
# THE
# SOPHIE TUCKER
# PERSONAL PHOTO ALBUM
# FROM HER GOLDEN JUBILEE

To
Marion, Milton
Judy, Lois
Young — with love to all
Sophie Tucker
May 17/54

*FIFTY GOLDEN YEARS*

LIMITED EDITION    Copy Number 672

Ted Shapiro — my pal
and music-man
for 34 of the 50 years.

The greatest of 'em all —
Mr. Words-and-Music
Himself — Irving Berlin

Sophie Tucker      Ted Lewis
White House
Washington, D.C.

— after telling President
Harding how to run
the country

*Little Judy Garland, my Beloved Fannie Brice and Harry Rapf — at M.G.M. Studios*

*"Soph" he says "Big things made us both famous."*

*with a couple of all-time movie greats"*

*This could be "Mister Bugel, make it legal"— but it's Mister Jessel.*

To, Mr. Winchell
I am not expecting the stork.

# INDEX

Printed in the United States
3006